D1560236

The Food and Wine of the North Fork

Historical Anecdotes and Recipes

The Food and Wine of the North Fork

Historical Anecdotes and Recipes

John Ross

Maple Hill Press

Back cover photo: Christian Di Lalla

Printed in the United States of America

ISBN 0-930545-24-9

Acknowledgments

This book is a labor of love that had its beginnings in 1973. Many people have helped me along the way and I owe them a debt of gratitude. First of all my wife Lois. She had to constantly adapt our family life to fit my impossible working schedule. My children, Sanford, Stewart, and Sarah, supported me by making our restaurant their home. I am thankful that my mother, Helen Ross, made it possible to start our business on the North Fork. Our recipes were kept in looseleaf notebooks by Bonnie Hoffner, who constantly edited them over the years. Without her this book would not have been possible. The names, dates, and historical anecdotes have come from interviews with restaurant people and their families. The Suffolk County Historical Society, The Southold Free Library, and The Cutchogue Free Library were sources for material, as well as *The Suffolk Times* and *The Traveler-Watchman*. I have taken many photographs myself, but some were contributed by Christian DiLalla, an employee of mine as a teenager but now a renowned professional photographer in Manhattan.

For the Greenport section, I would like to thank Bill Claudio, Ritchie Sledjeski, Ray and Dolly LaRiviere, Jack Levin and his daughters Rachel and Ellen, Gary Ostroski, Bruce Bollman, Brian Kavanagh, Aldo Maiorana, Jim Dubovick, Bobby Heaney, Dennis McDermott, Erik Orlowski, Claudia Helinski, and Rosa Ross. For the Orient section, my thanks to George Giannaris in East Marion and Bob Haase in Orient. For the Southold section, I am grateful to the Lieblein family, Christine Lauber, Carol and Greg Power, Billy Berliner, the Pavlou family, and Jenny Bienias. In Cutchogue, my thanks to Steve Abbott and Dan Reyburn; in New Suffolk, to Diane Harkoff and Elaine Romagnoli; in Mattituck, to Barbara Swahn, Skip Schoenhaur, Stephan Mazella, and Ettore Pennacchia. In Jamesport, Matt Kar, Bob Patchell, Cliff Saunders, and Neal Kopp; and in Aquebogue, the Wittmeier family and Tom Drake.

I am grateful to Jimmy Homan and Lloyd Corwin for providing historical background and pictures in the seafood and duck sections. Early inspiration for restaurant history came from Norm and Linda McCullough, Chris and Ros Baiz, Troy Gustavson, Bob Feger, Teresa Taylor, and Susan Whitney Simm. Antonia and Whitney Booth provided valuable historical facts and much support. Clifford Utz contributed restaurant history from his many bartending jobs.

Completion of this project would not have been possible without the advice of publishing professional Jean Marie Pierson. Graphic artist Kathryn Rempe did the word processing, the original layouts, and the scanning. My thanks for her patience during constant revisions. Michael and Rita Hagerman, owners of Academy Printing, have been a continuing source of support. Finally, I am grateful to Julie Fleck, President of Maple Hill Press, for completion and publication of this book.

Table of Contents

We may live without poetry,
music, and art;
We may live without conscience,
and live without heart;
We may live without friends,
We may live without books;
But civilized man cannot live
without cooks.
He may live without books —
What is knowledge but grieving?
He may live without hope —
What is hope but deceiving?
He may live without love —
What is passion but pining?
But where is the man that can
live without dining?

George Meredith
1828 - 1909

FOREWORD

It was late in 1973 when Lois and I, our 3-year-old son, Sanford, and our miniature schnauzer Leonard, first came to the North Fork. We were driving a 1970 Dodge Dart and had just left Ithaca, where I had recently graduated from the Cornell Hotel School. I was full of brash confidence and eager to own the riskiest business in the world — a restaurant.

We had settled on a place on the Main Road in Southold, across from the Wayside Market. It was called The Carriage House at the time and was owned by a fellow Cornellian, Stephen Mutkoski. It had, for a long time before that, been a restaurant called Jimmy's. We renamed it Ross' North Fork Restaurant.

It was also in 1973 that a young, somewhat eccentric graduate of Princeton and Harvard, Alex Hargrave, along with his wife Louisa, was planting the first modern vineyard on Long Island — Hargrave Vineyard. The excitement that the young couple generated about the possibility of distinctive, world-class Long Island wine is now history. But I'm getting ahead of myself here.

We decided to take a drive east on Route 25 to check out our competition. As we left Riverhead, we noticed Demkin's Duck Farm on the right (now Kmart and BJ's). We would buy ducks from them in the future.

As we drove into Aquebogue — the first village really situated on the North Fork — we saw the Modern Snack Bar on the left, with its classic 1950s neon sign.

Next came Brasby's. The place was big and ugly but it had lots of parking. Brasby's was popular for its Sunday Buffet, at the center of which was a huge steamship round of beef set up on its hipbone with the shank serving as a handle for carving. (I think the buffet price was $5.95 per person!)

Just past Brasby's was Little Joe's, a reliable Italian-style eatery where Joe and Kay greeted and served you clams oreganata, lasagna, spaghetti, veal parmesan, and cheesecake. In the next village, Jamesport, we passed the Elbow Room, known for its steaks and owned by Cliff Saunders. His concept involved buying choice short loins of beef and fabricating them into T-bones, strip steaks, and hamburger. He then invented a secret marinade. This idea was hugely popular and was copied by many North Fork restaurateurs for years to come.

Taking a short detour off the Main Road, we headed down to the water in New Suffolk where the Galley Ho, a classic fisherman's bar, served simple food. Across the street was Captain Ahab's.

Back on the Main Road, we continued east into Mattituck where we came upon Chez Nous, the only French restaurant on the North Fork. The owner was from Brooklyn, but his wife came from Quebec. He served sweetbreads, creme brulée, and escargots, and he always had a special bottle of wine "just for you." The Apple Tree was the casual place in Mattituck, and down by the inlet was the Old Mill Inn. It was right next to the Anchor Inn, which burned down later in the '70s.

In Cutchogue there was Fishermen's Rest. It had an active bar and booths along the wall where they served pizza, subs and heroes. It was usually very busy.

As we passed through Peconic and noticed Farmer Mike's farmstand and all the farmland, we thought there might be an opportunity here to cook fresh, local food from scratch without having to rely on trucked-in ingredients. The potatoes, cauliflower, tomatoes and other produce could be combined with the duck and all kinds of local seafood. We could even bring in some New York wine from the Finger Lakes, I remember thinking.

As we traveled east from our new restaurant in Southold and passed by Mullen Motors on the right, we saw the old Southold Inn. It was a sleepy looking place serving Italian food. But as we reached the water we came upon the most successful culinary tourist destination on the North Fork — Armando Cappa's Seafood Barge. Armando's mother would open in the morning and bake the pies and wash the windows facing the bay. There were four window tables and they were "turned" many times on a busy day. Armando had up to 22 waitresses and might do 1200 covers on a single day. His secret? Clams on paper plates, French fries and cole slaw as the only side dishes and *lots* of fried fish. He also served steamed oversized lobsters. Customers were intimidated to eat fast. But they seemed to love it.

Entering Greenport, we came to Mitchell's on the right on Front Street. It had the look of an old '50s restaurant with a huge square dining room. You just knew they had prime rib, baked potatoes in foil and iceberg lettuce salads on the menu. The famous rectangular bar was the centerpiece, decorated with old photos and illuminated by an antique Tiffany light.

Up on the North Road in Greenport were arch-rivals Soundview Inn and Porky's. Soundview was owned by Jack Levin, and had a spectacular view of Long Island Sound. Porky's was owned by the colorful Walter Sledjeski and was very busy in the mid-'70s. The portions were huge, and service was carried out by his veteran staff who, though efficient and friendly, were sometimes a little rough around the edges.

And down on the waterfront in Greenport, of course, was Claudio's, the oldest restaurant in America.

All of these restaurants were successful. Some had even achieved "institution" status, but they were getting a little tired as were many restaurants around the country at the time. The independently-owned and operated "family" restaurant was becoming an endangered species, or so it seemed, with the ever-growing chain restaurant business.

Today we are seeing renewed interest in local ingredients. The East End wineries have to be given much credit for this. Talented chefs and sophisticated diners are arriving each season to explore the expanding world of North Fork food and wine.

The following collection of recipes was taken from our notebooks at Ross' North Fork Restaurant and The Rotisserie between 1974 and 2004. I hope that you will use them as a guide to stimulate your imagination and share the enjoyment that I have experienced over the past thirty years.

Bon appetit!

— John Ross

PART ONE

RECIPES

The Long Island Oyster and Its Fellow Mollusks

How the word oyster is said:

French: Huitre

Dutch: Oester

German: Auster

Polish: Ostryga

Russian: Ustritsa

Chesapeake Bay Waterman: Arster

A Royal Royster with the Oyster

Let us royster with the oyster - in the shorter days and moister,

That are brought by brown September, with its roguish final R;

For breakfast or for supper, on the under shell or upper,

Of dishes he's the daisy, and of shell-fish he's the star.

We try him as they fry him, and even as they pie him;

We're partial to him luscious in a roast;

We boil and broil him, we vinegar-and-oil him,

And O he is delicious stewed with toast. .

We eat him with tomatoes, and the salad with potatoes,

Nor look him o'er with horror when he follows the coldslaw;

And neither does he fret us if he marches after lettuce

And abreast of cayenne pepper when his majesty is raw.

So welcome with September to the knife and glowing ember,

Juicy darling of our dainties, dispossessor of the clam!

To the oyster, then, a hoister, with him a royal royster

We shall whoop it through the land of heathen jam!

Anonymous

The Detroit Free Press, October 12, 1889

3

The Oyster and the North Fork

Fish and shellfish have been important to the North Fork since the time of the Native Americans. We are surrounded by some of the world's best shellfishing waters.

The oyster was the first "farmed" seafood and it made a huge economic impact on our area. Thousands of acres of bay bottom were leased out by the town. Cultivation began after 1820. Oyster-men "planted" shells during the spring in the brackish waters along the Connecticut shoreline. Larvae would attach to these shells and the bottom shell would "curl." They were now called spat oysters (or seed oysters) and could be transported to the more saline and fertile waters of Peconic Bay.

It takes a seed oyster three months to reach one inch in length and four years to reach market size. On average, one bushel of seed oysters would yield four bushels of mature oysters.

By 1900 Greeport grew to prominence as the commercial center for oyster production. L.F. Terry founded the Greenport Oyster Co. in 1888. In 1934, Greenport had the Lester and Toner Co.; J. & J.W. Ellsworth; Cedar Island Oyster Co.; South Ferry Oyster Co.; Robert Utz & Sons; and the E.E. Ball Co.

Production peaked at almost 25 million pounds of oyster meats. Hundreds of people were employed as openers, handlers, captains and crews. By 1960 production dropped to one million pounds, and is very small today.

Currently, the Spat Program (Southold Project in Aquaculture Training), conducted by the Cornell Cooperative Extension Marine Program, has focused public awareness on the importance of shellfish to the North Fork.

Purchasing, Handling, and Preparing Oysters

There are four species of oysters available today: the Atlantic Oyster, the Pacific Oyster, the Olympia Oyster, and the European Oyster. The dark, flat shell and briny taste of the Eastern Oyster make it famous. It grows from New Orleans to Prince Edward Island and comes in many varieties based on location. The most famous is the Blue Point from Long Island. The Pacific Oysters are the most prolific on the West Coast. They have curly, striped shells and almost white meat. Place names include Kuamoto, Portuguese, and Westcott Bay. The Olympia Oyster is also found on the West Coast. It is only about two inches in length. The last species is the European oyster, often called the Belon oyster. It is flat with a mild flavor.

You can purchase oysters in the shell or shucked. Buy shell oysters when serving them on the half shell, either raw or cooked. They should be tightly closed, with a fresh briny aroma. All oysters should be from approved waters. Consuming any raw shellfish carries the risk of being infected by the hepatitis B virus. Cooking eliminates the risk. Use commercially shucked oysters only for cooked preparations.

Opening Oysters

The amateur cook usually tries to avoid shucking oysters, but with a little practice, anyone can do it. The safest and easiest method is called "billing" or "cracking." With a pair of pliers, break off the tip or the "bill" of the oyster. Insert a stiff, straight-bladed oyster knife and twist to remove the top shell. Cut under the meat to loosen it from the adductor muscle. (You may want to rinse the oyster under cold water to remove any shell fragments — although connoisseurs would object to losing natural juices.)

Professionals use a stiff curved-bladed oyster knife. Hold the oyster in a towel and insert the knife into the hinge, pushing downward as you twist. The top shell will pop off. Cut under the meat with a second motion.

When using oysters for cooking, they open easily if you put them in a hot oven (425°F) for a few minutes. Remove from oven, pop off the top shells and add prepared ingredients. Do this close to serving time.

Oysters on the Half Shell

Yield: 4 portions

Ingredients	Amounts
fresh Long Island oysters	24
cracked ice	1 quart
lemon wedges	4
parsley to garnish	4 sprigs

Procedure:

1. Rinse oysters under cold water. Scrub with brush if necessary.
2. Shuck oysters (see directions, p. 5) and place on sheet pan.
3. Crack ice: wrap cubes in towel and place them on a solid cutting board. Hit with side of meat cleaver or hammer. Place ice in soup bowls.
4. Put six oysters on cracked ice in soup bowl. Garnish with lemon wedge and parsley.

Traditional Sauces

Cocktail Sauce
  Combine ¾ cup of catsup with ¼ cup chili sauce. Add 1 tbsp. prepared horseradish, 1 tbsp. of lemon juice, a pinch of cayenne pepper and a few drops of Tabasco sauce. Mix and chill.

Sauce Mignonette
  Combine ¼ cup minced shallots with 1 tbsp. of chopped parsley. Add 1 tsp. of ground black pepper, 1 tsp. of coarse salt and ½ cup of white wine vinegar.

Ravigote Sauce
  Combine in food processor 1 cup chopped scallions, 1 tbsp. garlic, ¼ cup parsley, ¼ cup dill, 2 tbsp. capers, 2 tbsp. Dijon mustard, and ¼ cup white wine vinegar. Process one minute and gradually add ½ cup olive oil. Season with salt and pepper.

Recommended Wine: Sauvignon Blanc; crisp Chardonnay; sparkling wine.

Oysters Baked in Garlic and Pernod

Yield: 4 portions

Ingredients	Amounts
oysters, washed and opened as if for eating on the half shell	24
unsalted butter, melted	½ cup
garlic, minced	2 tbsp.
Pernod (anise flavored liqueur)	2 tbsp.
Italian flat leaf parsley, chopped	¼ cup
fresh bread crumbs (from day-old French bread, or Japanese panko)	½ cup
paprika	1 tbsp.
bacon, diced ¼" (pancetta or prosciutto make good . substitutes)	24 pieces
lemon wedges	8

Procedure:

1. Place oysters on sheet pan with sides. Pre-heat oven to 400°F.

2. Spoon melted butter over oysters. Sprinkle on garlic, Pernod, parsley, bread crumbs, and paprika.

3. Place a square of bacon on each oyster and roast in 400°F oven for 10 minutes or until bacon is lightly browned. Serve with lemon wedges.

Recommended Wine: Sauvignon Blanc; Riesling or crisp Chardonnay

Oysters Rockefeller

Yield: 4 portions (6 oysters each)

Ingredients	Amounts
oysters, on the half shell	24
spinach, coarsely chopped, loose	4 cups
scallion, cut in ¼" pieces	½ cup
romaine lettuce, coarsely chopped	2 cups
celery, diced	½ cup
parsley, coarsely chopped	½ cup
garlic, coarsely chopped	1 tbsp.
butter (or olive oil)	¼ cup
bread crumbs	½ cup
Worcestershire sauce	1 tsp.
anchovy, minced	1 tsp.
Tabasco sauce	few drops
Pernod	1 tbsp.

Procedure:

1. Open fresh oysters (see instructions, p.5) and place them on a sheet pan.

2. Combine spinach, scallion, lettuce, celery, parsley, and garlic into a bowl of a food processor and pulse until finely chopped. (If desired, this can be done by hand with a chef's knife).

3. In a saute pan, heat the butter or oil and add the chopped greens. Stir in the bread crumbs, Worcestershire, anchovy, Tabasco, and Pernod. Taste for seasoning.

4. Spoon mixture over oysters and bake in 400° oven for 10 minutes. Serve with lemon wedges.

Sauteed Oysters Panko

Yield: about 6 portions of 4 oysters each

Ingredients	Amounts
shucked fresh oysters	1 pint
flour	2 cups
salt	1 tbsp.
pepper	1 tbsp.
eggs	2
milk	2 cups
Japanese bread crumbs (panko)	1 quart
olive oil	¼ cup
butter, unsalted	¼ cup
wasabi powder	¼ cup
cold water	2 tbsp.
lemon wedges	8

Procedure:

1. Place flour on sheet pan and season with salt and pepper.

2. Beat eggs in small bowl and stir in milk for egg wash.

3. Place panko in another sheet pan.

4. Dredge oysters in flour, soak in egg wash, and bread in panko. Place oysters on clean sheet pan.

5. Heat olive oil and butter in saute pan. Cook oysters over medium heat until golden brown.

6. Dissolve wasabi in cold water and serve on the side with lemon wedges.

Note: Serve over baby arugula. If desired, these oysters can be deep fried.

Recommended Wine: Sauvignon Blanc or crisp Chardonnay

Pan Roasted Oysters over Toast Points

Yield: 4 portions

Ingredients	Amounts
shucked fresh oysters	1 pint
paprika	1 tbsp.
celery salt	1 tsp.
ground black pepper	1 tsp.
butter	2 tbsp.
chili sauce	½ cup
lemon juice	1 tsp.
Worcestershire sauce	1 tsp.
Tabasco sauce	¼ tsp.
sour cream	½ cup
dry sherry	1 tbsp.
toast points	6 slices toast, quartered

Procedure:

1. In saucepan, cook oysters in their own juice about one minute or until edges just begin to curl.

2. Transfer to plate with a slotted spoon and discard liquid.

3. Melt butter in same pan and add paprika, celery salt, and pepper. Stir. Add oysters and stir to coat.

4. Add chili sauce, lemon juice, Worcestershire sauce and tabasco. Stir and bring to boil.

5. Stir in sour cream and sherry and serve over toast points.

Notes: This dish is good as an hors d'oeuvre when served in bread croustades. Purchase soft white bread (such as Wonder Bread) and cut 3" rounds with cookie cutter. Paint small (1½") muffin tins with melted butter. Press bread into muffin tins and bake at 400° for 5 minutes. Cool. Place one oyster and a little sauce in each croustade.

Recommended Wine: A crisp Chardonnay.

This recipe is an adaptation of the famous recipe from the Grand Central Oyster Bar.

Scalloped Oysters and Potatoes

Yield: 4 portions

Ingredients	Amounts
Long Island potatoes	2 lbs.
Japanese bread crumbs (panko)	2 cups
shucked oysters	1 pint
chopped parsley	¼ cup
chopped onion	1 cup
cold, unsalted butter	¼ cup
coarse salt	1 tbsp.
ground black pepper	1 tbsp.
nutmeg	1 tsp.
heavy cream	2 cups
paprika	1 tbsp.

Procedure:

1. Boil potatoes in their skins until just cooked. Cool, peel.

2. Rub a rectangular baking pan with butter and sprinkle bottom with a layer of Japanese bread crumbs (panko).

3. Slice potatoes and place one layer on top of crumbs. Place a layer of oysters on potatoes and sprinkle with parsley, onion, salt, pepper, and nutmeg. Slice small pieces of butter on top.

4. Repeat step 3. Sprinkle Japanese bread crumbs on top and pour in heavy cream. Garnish with paprika and cook, uncovered, in a 350° oven for 30 minutes.

Recommended Wine: Barrel Fermented Chardonnay

11

Quahaugs – Littlenecks, Cherrystones and Chowders

The term Clamdigger is broadly used, applying not only to those who dig 'em but also to those who rake, tong, dredge and tread. And speaking of the latter school —

> There's an old belief that a Shinnecock chief
> First introduced the role,
> Of treading clams, that sport of hams
> Who seek a cleaner sole
> And who know the savage thrill of it,
> The aboriginal skill of it —
> To tramp around in bottom mud
> Telling the real clam from the dud.
>
> This Shinnecock chief, to put it brief,
> Discovered his technique
> When staggering back from a midnight snack
> He tumbled into a creek,
> And when upon its muddy bottom
> His feet struck clams, he stooped and gottom,
> Carried them safely to the medder
> And thus became the world's first treader.
>
> You don't tread clams just for the clams
> Unless it's your vacation
> But you can run a marathon
> And stay in one location,
> And then there is the glee of it,
> The sort of corps de sprit of it,—
> To snare the unsuspecting clam
> By stepping on its diaphragm.
>
> That picture called September Morn
> Has gotten lots of slams
> Because folks just don't realize
> The lady's treading clams.
> With one foot on the shell of it,
> She's poised, and that's the hell of it,
> Hoping before she makes the grab
> It ain't another gol-durned crab.

From *Historic Long Island,* 1956, by Paul Bailey
Courtesy of Suffolk County Historical Society

Baked Clams Casino

Yield: 4 portions

Ingredients	Amounts
Littleneck clams, washed and opened as if for eating on the half shell.	24
unsalted butter, softened	1½ cups
shallots, minced	2 tbsp.
green pepper, finely diced	¼ cup
red pepper, finely diced	¼ cup
fresh horseradish, shredded	1 tbsp.
kosher salt	1 tsp.
Worcestershire sauce	1 tbsp.
Tabasco sauce	½ tsp.
paprika	1 tsp.
lemon juice	1 tbsp.
Italian flat leaf parsley, chopped	1 tbsp.
bacon, cut in ¼" squares	24 squares

Procedure:

1. Begin by making casino butter. Place softened butter in a bowl and add all ingredients except for bacon. Combine with a wooden spoon. Form this mixture into a cylinder on a rectangle of aluminum foil. Roll up the foil around the butter mixture and squeeze it into a roll about 6" long and 1" in diameter. Refrigerate.

2. Place opened clams on a sheet pan and preheat oven to 400°F.

3. Remove casino butter from refrigerator and slice into 24 rounds. Place one on top of each clam.

4. Top clams with bacon squares and roast for 10 minutes in hot oven.

Recommended Wine: Barrel Fermented Chardonnay

Baked Stuffed Cherrystone Clams

Yield: 30 clams or 6 portions

Ingredients	Amounts
cherrystone clams	15
butter	2 tbsp.
onions, finely chopped	1 cup
garlic, minced	1 tbsp
mushrooms, finely chopped	2 cups
oregano	1 tbsp
ground black pepper	1 tsp
chopped parsley	¼ cup
butter	½ cup
flour	⅔ cup
milk	1 cup
reserved clam juice	1 cup
bread crumbs	about 1½ cups
grated Parmesan cheese	½ cup
paprika	1 tbsp.
lemon wedges	8

Procedure:

1. Wash clams and open, reserving juice, shells, and clams.

2. Boil shells to sterilize, and chop clams. Set aside.

3. Melt butter in saute pan and add onions, garlic, mushrooms, oregano and black pepper. Cook about 5 minutes and add parsley and chopped clams. Cook another 5 minutes and set aside.

4. In saucepan, melt butter and stir in flour to make roux. Whisk in milk and clam juice and bring to a boil (sauce will be very thick).

5. Combine sauce with clam mixture in saute pan. Stir in breadcumbs until no liquid is left.

6. Rinse clam shells in cold water and stuff with clam mixture. Sprinkle cheese and paprika over them and refrigerate.

7. At service time, put clams in a 400°F oven on a sheet pan and cook about 10 minutes. Serve with lemons.

Note: Japanese bread crumbs (panko) are a good substitute for plain bread crumbs.

Recommended Wine: Crisp Chardonnay

North Fork Creamy Clam Chowder
Yield: 2 quarts or 8 portions

Ingredients	Amounts
chowder clams	12
bacon, diced	2 strips
onion, diced	½ cup
new potatoes, peeled and diced	2 cups
parsnips, peeled, diced	1 cup
garlic, minced	1 tbsp.
heavy cream	1 pint
milk	1 quart
clam juice	2 cups
butter, melted	½ cup
flour	½ cup
freshly ground pepper	1 tsp.
salt	1 tsp.
thyme	1 tbsp.

Procedure:

1. Open clams, reserving juice. Chop clams and set aside.

2. Brown bacon in saute pan. Add onions and cook briefly.

3. Transfer onions and bacon to double boiler. Add potatoes, parsnips, garlic and cream. Cook, covered, in double boiler for one hour.

4. Heat milk and clam juice in separate pan. Combine melted butter and flour to make a roux. Add to milk/clam juice mixture. Add this to double boiler along with chopped clams. Add seasoning and cook 15 minutes.

Note: If chowder clams are difficult to open, place them in a bowl and cover them with hot water. Let sit for 5 minutes and open.

Bonac Clam Chowder

Yield: 2 quarts or 8 portions

Ingredients	Amounts
chowder clams	12
bacon, diced	2 strips
onions, coarsely chopped	2 cups
potatoes, peeled, cut up	1 quart
carrot, peeled, cut up	1 cup
celery, cut up	1 cup
juice from clams + water	2 quarts
canned tomatoes, chopped	1 cup
thyme	1 tsp.
black pepper	1 tsp.
Old Bay Seafood seasoning	1 tsp.

Procedure:

1. Open clams, reserving juice.

2. Dice bacon and brown in soup pot.

3. Using meat grinder, grind onion, potato, carrot, and celery. (You may substitute food processor. If so, pulse quickly until chopped.)

4. Add ground vegetables plus clam juice and water to bacon. Cook for half an hour.

5. Put shucked clams through meat grinder and add to chowder.

6. Add tomatoes and seasonings. Simmer 15 minutes.

Note: The meat grinder produces a rice-like texture in this soup which gives it its character. If chowder clams are difficult to open, place them in a bowl and cover them with hot water. Let sit for 5 minutes and open.

This is an adaptation of an old Depression-era recipe. It comes from a book titled *From Alewives to Whelks*. "Bonac" refers to the nickname given to people from East Hampton: Bonackers.

Creamy Clam and Mussel Soup
Yield: 8 Portions, about 2 quarts

Ingredients	Amounts
Littleneck clams	2 dozen
mussels	2 dozen
butter	¼ cup
chopped leeks	½ cup
chopped shallots	½ cup
chopped garlic	2 tbsp.
Chardonnay	2 cups
chopped parsley	½ cup
water	1 cup
heavy cream	2 cups
salt and pepper	as needed

Procedure:

1. Wash clams and mussels.

2. Melt butter in soup pot and add leeks, shallots, and garlic, cook for one minute.

3. Add Chardonnay and half of the parsley, and bring to boil; reduce liquid by one-third.

4. Add clams, mussels and water, cover, and cook until shellfish opens.

5. Remove clams and mussels and add cream, salt and pepper.

6. Remove mussels and clams from shells, add back to soup and garnish with remaining parsley.

Note: Leave a few clams and mussels in the shell. Put them in each bowl of soup as a garnish.

Recommended Wine: Chardonnay

17

Peconic Bay Scallops

The Peconic Bay scallop is one of the best mollusks in the world and part of what makes the North Fork a great culinary region. Jimmy Homan, owner of Braun Seafood Co., was a prime influence in the success of this precious shellfish.

In 1949, when Jim Homan joined Captain George Braun, the business consisted of oyster farming and a side business of fishing bait. Jim would drive to New York and return with truckloads of worms. He later expanded to frozen bait, such as squid and sand eels. But by 1959, when Jimmy Homan bought out George Braun, he was building an ever-expanding seafood company.

Braun Seafood Co., Cutchogue

In 1962, Braun's marketed about 300,000 pounds of Bay scallops. Jim had an office in Greenport and another in Cutchogue where they would buy scallops from hundreds of baymen. They also had buyers in Sag Harbor and Amagansett. The going wholesale price averaged $0.73 per pound. (By 2002, the total harvest had dropped to 2,300 pounds with a wholesale price of $17.69/lb.)

During the '60s and '70s, Braun's shipped a large percentage of their harvest to the Boston market. They also supplied many New York City restaurants, such as Luchow's, the "21 Club" and Schrafft's, as well as restaurants on Long Island such as the Seascape, Thatched Cottage, Mitchell's in Greenport, and the Yankee Clipper.

When available, fresh scallops from Peconic Bay are the best in the world. Their delicate flavor and juicy texture need little help from the chef. Here are some simple and classic recipes.

Bay Scallop Saute

Yield: 4 portions

Ingredients	Amounts
Peconic Bay scallops	1½ lbs.
unsalted butter	½ cup
Kosher salt	1 tsp.
freshly ground pepper	½ tsp.
lemon, cut in wedges	1
chopped parsley	2 tbsp.

Procedure:

1. Heat butter in saute pan until it foams and just begins to brown. Add scallops and cook at high heat for two minutes. Shake pan (Do not crowd scallops — cook in batches or use a large pan.)

2. Add salt, pepper to pan. Squeeze lemon wedges into pan and add parsley. Serve immediately.

Recommended Wine: Riesling; Pinot Blanc or Sauvignon Blanc.

Peconic Bay Scallops — Beurre Blanc

Yield: 4 portions

Ingredients	Amounts
Peconic Bay scallops	1½ lbs.
shallots, finely chopped	½ cup
Sauvignon Blanc	¼ cup
fresh lemon juice	2 tbsp.
unsalted butter, cold, cut in pieces	1 cup
salt	1 tsp.
pepper	½ tsp.
chopped parsley	¼ cup

Procedure:

1. In saute pan combine shallots, wine, and lemon juice. Bring to a boil and add scallops. Cook about two minutes and remove scallops with slotted spoon. Reduce liquid by two-thirds.

2. Remove from heat and whisk in cold butter. Strain over scallops and garnish with parsley. Season with salt and pepper.

Recommended Wine: Sauvignon Blanc

Pan Seared Sea Scallops with Lime

Yield: 4 portions

Ingredients	Amounts
fresh sea scallops	1 lb.
extra virgin olive oil	¼ cup
flour	1 cup
salt	1 tsp.
pepper	1 tsp.
fresh lime juice	1 tbsp.
Rose's lime juice	1 tbsp.
baby spinach (or other fresh greens)	4 oz.
chopped parsley	¼ cup

Procedure:

1. Combine flour, salt, pepper, in bowl. Toss scallops in flour and shake off excess. (If desired, use sieve)

2. Heat heavy saute pan very hot, add a little olive oil and one layer of scallops (leave space between them). Cook until rich brown color develops on one side (2 minutes), loosen with spatula and add the fresh lime juice and Rose's lime juice (the bottled juice contains sugar which quickly carmelizes). Toss quickly and remove from heat. Repeat cooking in batches.

3. Serve scallops over wilted greens. Garnish with fresh lime and chopped parsley.

Note: If sea scallops are large, cut in half horizontally.

Recommended Wine: Sauvignon Blanc or dry Riesling

Peconic Bay Scallop Seviche

Yield: 4 appetizer portions

Ingredients	Amounts
Peconic Bay scallops (very fresh)	1 lb.
fresh lime juice	½ cup
Jalapeño pepper, minced	1
red onion, finely diced	½ cup
fresh cilantro, minced	1 tbsp.
extra virgin olive oil.	1 tbsp.
fresh tomato, peeled, seeded, chopped	½ cup
garlic, minced	1 tsp.
coarse salt	1 tsp.
ground pepper	1 tsp.

Procedure:

Combine all ingredients in a stainless steel bowl and refrigerate at least four hours. Scallops will turn opaque. Serve over fresh arugula with lime.

Recommended Wine: Gewurztraminer

Coquilles Saint Jacques à la Parisienne
Yield: 4 portions

Ingredients	Amounts
Peconic Bay scallops	1½ lbs.
(with 4 scallop shells)	
small white mushrooms sliced	8 oz.
butter	2 tbsp.
lemon juice	1 tbsp.
heavy cream	½ cup
soft butter and flour kneaded together	1 tbsp. of each
salt, pepper	to taste
Yukon Gold potatoes	1 lb.
egg yolk	1
butter	1 tbsp.
grated Gruyere or Swiss cheese	½ cup
bread crumbs	¼ cup
paprika	1 tsp.

Procedure:

1. Melt 2 tbsp. of butter in saute pan and add 1 tbsp. of lemon juice. Add scallops and cook until just opaque, about five minutes. Remove with slotted spoon. Add sliced mushrooms to pan and cook briefly. Remove with slotted spoon.
2. Reduce liquid in pan by half and add ½ cup of heavy cream. Season with salt and pepper and thicken with kneaded balls of flour and butter (beurre manie); the sauce should be medium thick.
3. Peel potatoes, cut up and boil until fully cooked. Mash with butter, one egg yolk, and salt and pepper. Place in pastry bag with star tube.
4. Place scallop shells on sheet pan. Line bottom with layer of sliced mushrooms. Place scallops on top. Pour sauce over scallops and sprinkle with grated Gruyere or Swiss cheese. Pipe potatoes around edge of shells. Sprinkle top with a few fresh bread crumbs and a little paprika.
5. Put scallops in a hot oven or low broiler and cook until cheese browns and sauce bubbles.

Note: You can substitute a ceramic ramekin for scallop shells.

Recommended Wine: Barrel Fermented Chardonnay.

Steamed Mussels in White Wine
(Moules Marniere)
Yield: 4 portions

Ingredients	Amounts
mussels, fresh in shell	3 lb.
shallots, finely chopped	½ cup
parsley stems	6
bay leaf	1
thyme	1 tsp.
fresh ground pepper	1 tsp.
Long Island Chardonnay	1 cup
chopped parsley	¼ cup
cold butter	2 oz.
lemon juice	1 tbsp.

Procedure:

1. Wash mussels under cold water. Most commercial mussels are now farmed and often come from Prince Edward Island. They are very clean. But some chefs like to soak mussels and clams in brine (one-third cup salt to one gallon water) to get rid of sand. Adding cornstarch to the water will help also.

2. Place mussels in stock pot and add shallots, parsley stems, bay leaf, thyme, pepper and Chardonnay. Cover and bring to a boil. Cook until shells open, about five minutes.

3. Strain the broth into a saucepan and bring it to a boil. Let it boil about five minutes, reducing liquid. Stir in parsley, butter, and lemon juice. Taste for seasoning.

4. Arrange mussels on the half shell in shallow bowls. Pour sauce over them.

Mussels Provençale:

Follow the above recipe, substituting red wine for white. Omit the thyme. Add ½ cup chopped garlic. After straining broth, stir in 2 tbsp. tomato paste with the butter and parsley. Sprinkle parmesan cheese over mussels when serving.

Recommended Wine: A crisp Chardonnay

24

Curried Mussels with Pistachio Nuts

Yield: 4 portions

Ingredients	Amounts
mussels, fresh in shell	3 lbs.
shallots, finely chopped	¼ cup
parsley stems	6
bay leaf	1
thyme	1 tsp.
black pepper	1 tsp.
white wine	½ cup
onion, diced	½ cup
celery, diced	½ cup
butter	2 oz.
curry powder	1 tbsp.
flour	¼ cup
mussel broth	1 cup
apple, peeled, cored, diced	1 cup
golden raisins	½ cup
pistachio nuts	½ cup
chopped parsley	¼ cup
heavy cream	1 cup
lemon juice	1 tbsp.
pepper	1 tsp.

Procedure:

1. Place mussels in stock pot and add next six ingredients. Bring to boil and cook until shells open, about 5 min. Strain broth and reserve. Let mussels cool and remove them from the shells.

2. Melt butter in sauce pan and add onion and celery. When soft, stir in curry powder and flour. Stir in mussel broth and bring to a boil.

3. Stir in apples, raisins, pistachio nuts and parsley. Add heavy cream and lemon juice. Check for seasoning and fold in mussels. Serve in small bowls as appetizer or with steamed rice as an entree.

Recommended Wine: Gewurztraminer

The Crustaceans: Lobster and Shrimp

Photo taken at Ross' North Fork Restauarant by
Appellation Magazine, August 1997.
Photographer: Andre Baranowski

Summer Lobster Stew

Yield: 4 portions

Ingredients	Amounts
lobsters, live	4 1¼ lb. lobsters
onions, diced	2 cups
leeks, white part diced	1 cup
butter	½ cup
fresh thyme, chopped	2 tbsp
red pepper, diced	1 cup
green pepper, diced	1 cup
flour	½ cup
chicken stock	3 cups
corn on the cob	4 ears
new potatoes, peeled, cooked (left whole if small)	8
sugar snap peas	2 cups
Italian parsley	¼ cup
heavy cream	1 cup
salt and ground pepper	to taste

Procedure:

1. Boil lobsters in large pot until just cooked (about 20 min). Remove and cool. Remove meat and cut it in bite sized chunks. Leave claw meat whole. Boil potatoes in lobster broth and set aside.

2. Melt butter in soup pot and add onions and leeks. Cook for 3 minutes and add peppers. Saute another 3 minutes. Stir in flour.

3. Stir in chicken stock and bring to a boil. Sauce should be lightly thickened.

4. Add new potatoes and simmer about 15 minutes.

5. Scrape kernels off corn with a paring knife. Add to sauce along with sugar snap peas, fresh thyme, and parsley. Cook about 5 min.

6. Stir in heavy cream and lobster meat.

7. Check for seasoning and serve in soup bowls.

Notes: This dish is called "summer" lobster stew because all of the ingredients are available locally and very fresh during July and August. Barrel fermented Long Island Chardonnay and French bread must be served with this meal. If it is too late for local sugar snap peas, substitute green beans. Corn must be just picked.

Baked Stuffed Lobster

Yield: 4 portions

Ingredients	Amounts
live lobsters 1½ - 2 lbs.	4
butter	½ cup
bread crumbs	1 cup
meat from legs, chopped	
coral, chopped	
tomalley, chopped	
Worcestershire sauce	1 tbsp.
sherry	2 tbsp.
salt/pepper	1 tbsp.
butter, melted	¼ cup

Procedure:

1. Split lobsters in half but do not cut through back completely. Remove head sac and throw away. Remove coral and tomalley and reserve. Cut off small legs along sides of lobsters.

2. Boil legs for 10 minutes, and cool. Remove meat and chop. Chop coral and tomalley. Melt butter in saute pan and add breadcrumbs. Cook until lightly browned and add coral, tomalley, lobster meat, Worcestershire, and sherry. Season with salt and pepper and stuff in body cavity of lobster.

3. Place lobsters on sheet pan, weight tails down (if possible — it's not essential), brush with melted butter, and roast in a 425°F oven about 25 minutes, or until meat is firm and opaque.

Notes: The legs of small lobsters do not contain much meat, but on 2-lb. lobsters it's enough to be worthwhile. Other shellfish such as shrimp or scallops can be added to this stuffing.

In the '60s and '70s, very few lobsters were steamed in restaurants on Long Island. Most were "broiled" or baked stuffed.

Recommended Wine: Barrel Fermented Chardonnay

Lobster Thermidor

Yield: 4 portions

Ingredients	Amounts
live lobsters, 1¼ lb	4
olive oil	2 tbsp.
mushrooms, quartered	2 cups
butter	4 oz.
lemon juice	1 tsp.
salt	½ tsp.
shallots, chopped fine	½ cup
Pernod	1 tbsp.
white wine	1 cup
tarragon	1 tsp.
heavy cream	1 cup
cayenne pepper	pinch
Parmesan cheese	½ cup
paprika	1 tbsp.

Procedure:

1. Split lobsters in half lengthwise. Remove head sacs and discard. Remove coral and tomalley and set aside. Boil claws until they turn red. Cool and remove meat.
2. Saute lobsters in olive oil, shell side down, until they turn red and meat is just cooked. Remove and set aside.
3. Pour off excess oil and add 2 tbsp. of butter and lemon juice to pan. Saute quartered mushrooms and remove.
4. Remove meat from lobster shells and cut into ½" chunks. Rinse shells and set aside.
5. Add 2 tbsp. butter to saute pan along with ¼ cup shallots, salt, Pernod and all lobster meat. Return mushrooms to pan and cook for 2 minutes.
6. In a saucepan add white wine and 2 tbsp. chopped shallots. Reduce by half. Stir in heavy cream, cayenne pepper, and chopped coral and tomalley. Add to the lobster mixture. Stir and season.
7. Place this mixture back in shells. Sprinkle with parmesan and paprika and place in hot oven until golden brown.

Note: Like Lobster Newburg, this was a classic restaurant item in the '70s. This recipe calls for sauteing live lobster and using the pan drippings for extra flavor.

Recommended Wine: Barrel Fermented Chardonnay

Lobster Newburg

Yield: 4 portions

Ingredients	Amounts
cooked lobster meat cut in ½" chunks	1 lb.
butter	2 tbsp.
paprika	1 tbsp.
dry sherry	2 tbsp.
lemon juice	1 tbsp.
heavy cream	1½ cups
salt	1 tsp.
pepper, white	½ tsp.
puff pastry shells	4

Procedure:

1. Melt butter in saute pan and add lobster meat. Add paprika, sherry and lemon juice and cook slowly.

2. Stir in heavy cream and season with salt and white pepper.

3. Serve over puff pastry shells or toast points (see recipe for puff pastry, p. 95), or use frozen puff pastry squares.

Notes: Lobster Newburg was a classic restaurant menu item in the '60s and '70s. It often degenerated into a way to use not very fresh leftovers. When made with just-cooked lobster it is delicious. In order to get one pound of lobster meat, you will need four 1¼ lb. live lobsters.

Recommended Wine: Barrel Fermented Chardonnay

Roasted Winter Beets with Lobster

Yield: 4 Portions

Ingredients	Amounts
winter beets, 4" in diameter	4
1¼ lb. lobsters, live	4
minced shallots	¼ cup
white wine	½ cup
orange juice	½ cup
lemon juice	2 tbsp.
heavy cream	1 cup
butter, unsalted	4 oz.
orange zest	2 tbsp.
orange slices, peeled	8
salt	1 tsp.
white pepper	½ tsp.

Procedure:

1. Roast unpeeled beets in a 300° oven for one hour. Pierce with a small knife to check tenderness. Remove beets and deglaze pan with ¼ cup water. Reserve juice.

2. Cook lobster in boiling salted water about 20 minutes. Cool under cold water and remove meat. Cut in bite sized chunks.

3. Peel beets and cut in half. Slice a small piece off bottom so that they stand flat. Hollow out center with melon baller. Use these balls as garnish.

4. In a small saucepan combine shallots, wine, orange juice, and lemon juice. Cook until reduced to ¼ cup. Add cream and whisk in small chunks of butter.

5. Strain this sauce into saute pan and add lobster chunks. Add beet deglazing liquid and orange zest. Season with salt and pepper.

6. Pour this mixture over warm beets and garnish with orange slices.

Note: The beet juice colors the sauce a perfect shade of pink. If you carve the beets into the shape of a heart, the dish is perfect for Valentine's.

Recommended Wine: Barrel Fermented Chardonnay

Shrimp in Ale Batter
With Horseradish Marmalade Sauce

Yield: 4 Portions

Ingredients	Amounts	
shrimp, raw, 16/20 size	20	
flour	1 cup	
salt	1 tsp.	
pepper	½ tsp.	batter
beer or ale	2 cups	
egg	1	
paprika	1 tbsp.	
flour	1 cup	
salt	1 tsp.	
pepper	1 tsp.	
orange marmalade	1 cup	
orange juice	¼ cup	
lemon juice	2 tbsp.	sauce
horseradish, prepared	2 tbsp.	
ginger, ground	1 tsp.	

Procedure:

1. Peel and devein shrimp, removing tails. Refrigerate.

2. Season flour and set aside.

3. In a small bowl, break one egg and whisk in beer. Gradually stir in flour until thickness of pancake batter is reached. Season with paprika, salt and pepper.

4. In another bowl, add orange juice and lemon juice to marmalade. Season with horseradish and ginger.

5. Heat oil in deep fryer to 350°. If you do not have a deep fryer, heat oil 3" deep in a heavy sauce pan to 350°.

6. Dredge shrimp in seasoned flour and individually dip them in batter with tongs. Hold them in the oil momentarily so they won't stick to each other. Cook about 3 minutes and remove. Serve with sauce.

Recommended Wine: Stainless Steel Fermented Chardonnay.

Shrimp Scampi

Yield: 4 Portions

Ingredients	Amounts
shrimp, raw, 16/20 size peeled, butterflied and deveined, tails left on	20

Scampi Butter:	
unsalted butter	½ lb.
shallots, minced	¼ cup
garlic, minced	2 tbsp.
parsley, chopped	¼ cup
lemon juice	1 tbsp.
sherry, dry	1 tbsp.
salt	1 tsp.
pepper	½ tsp.

Procedure:

1. Peel shrimp, leaving tails on. Make a deep cut along the back to butterfly. Remove vein and rinse shrimp.

2. Combine all ingredients for the scampi butter into a bowl. Allow butter to soften. Mix with a wooden spoon and transfer to a rectangular foil sheet. Roll the butter into a cylinder and refrigerate.

3. To cook, place shrimp in individual porcelain ramekins or into a baking dish. Slice pieces of scampi butter over shrimp and cook in 425° oven for 10 minutes or until pink. Serve over rice.

Note: If desired, cook shrimp in saute pan with scampi butter.

Recommended Wine: Stainless Steel Fermented Chardonnay

Sauteed Shrimp with Pesto and Fettuccine

Yield: 4 Portions

Ingredients	Amounts
shrimp, raw, 16/20 size	
peeled, deveined, tails removed	20
chef's salt*	1 tbsp.
extra virgin olive oil	¼ cup
garlic, minced	2 tbsp.
fresh tomato, peeled	
seeded, chopped	2 cups
white wine	½ cup
fresh basil, chopped	½ cup
pesto (see recipe next page)	½ cup
fettuccine, freshly made	
(see recipe, p. 36)	1 lb.
parmigiano-reggiano cheese	
grated fresh	½ cup

Procedure:

1. Heat oil in large sautoir. Add shrimp and chef's salt. Cook at high heat until shrimp are just cooked (about 3 min.). Remove shrimp with slotted spoon.

2. Add garlic, shallots, and tomato to pan and saute for 3 minutes. Add wine and bring to a boil.

3. Add shrimp along with basil and pesto. Cook until hot and serve over freshly made fettucine. Sprinkle cheese over each portion.

Recommended Wine: Stainless Steel Fermented Chardonnay

Note: Commercial pesto and fetuccine can be used, but the fresh homemade version lends an added dimension to the dish.

* Chef's salt: 1 cup coarse salt + ¼ cup freshly ground black pepper.

Pesto alla Genovese

Yield: 1½ - 2 cups

Ingredients	Amounts
fresh basil leaves washed, dried, stripped from stems, coarsely chopped and tightly packed	2 cups
salt	1 tsp
black pepper, fresh ground	½ tsp
garlic, minced	1 tbsp
pine nuts or walnuts, chopped	2 tbsp
olive oil	1 cup
Parmesan cheese	½ cup

Procedure:

1. Combine basil, salt, pepper, garlic, walnuts and ½ cup of oil in food processor. Pulse a few times, then process at high speed. Stop occasionally and scrape down herbs.

2. Add remaining oil. Sauce should be thin enough to run off the spatula easily.

3. Scrape sauce into plastic tub and stir in cheese.

Notes: To further thin the sauce at serving time, add a little spaghetti water. Serve pesto with homemade fettucine (see recipe, next page) and sauteed shrimp.

Homemade Fettuccine
Fresh Egg Pasta

Yield: About 1 pound pasta or 4 portions

Ingredients	Amounts
bread flour	1 cup
semolina (or cornmeal)	1 cup
eggs, lightly beaten	4
olive oil	1 tbsp.
salt	½ tsp.

Procedure:

1. Place all ingredients in bowl of food processor. Process until blended (it will look like coarse cornmeal). Remove and gather into a ball.

2. Knead for about ten minutes using the palm and heel of the hand. Use just a little flour to prevent sticking.

3. Cover with plastic wap and let it rest for half an hour.

Note: You may also use a mixer with a dough hook, or you can do the whole recipe with your hands. The important step is to knead it.

Making Fettuccine

1. Cut ball of pasta into quarters. Roll each one into a ball and set aside.

2. Take one small ball of pasta and roll it into a rectangle. If you have a mechanical pasta cutter, feed it into the machine. If you don't, roll it as thin as possible on a lightly floured board. Cut ¼" wide strips with a knife and hang them over a broomstick to dry. (If using machine, hang them on broomstick the same way). When all the pasta is cut and hanging, cook it very quickly in boiling salted water and drain. You may rinse it in cold water and store in a covered bowl in the refrigerator.

Long Island
Fin Fish

Long Island Flounder

Flounder has been the most popular local fish on the North Fork for years. The flavor is mild, it has a delicate texture, and it lends itself to many preparations. People who don't like seafood like it because it doesn't taste "fishy." Chefs like it because you can broil it, fry it, saute it, poach it, and bake it. It lends itself to many sauces and garnishes and it has always been modestly priced.

The flounder is a member of the flatfish family which includes the Dover sole in Europe and the Petrale sole on the West Coast. The winter flounder is the most important flounder and is marketed as "Flounder," "Blackback," and "Lemon Sole." The summer flounder is marketed as "Fluke." The witch flounder is marketed as "Gray Sole." The Atlantic Halibut is the largest member of the flatfish family.

Flounder is almost always purchased in boneless, skinless filets and should be bought fresh. Cook it just before serving and use delicate sauces and herbs. Flounder lends itself to wine cookery and goes very well with wine. The following recipes are flounder classics that don't seem to go out of style.

The Bay, the Sound, and the Atlantic Ocean are home to many other types of fish popular on the North Fork. Some, such as bluefish, blowfish, weakfish, and porgies, are more popular with sports fisherman than as commercial restaurant fish. In local restaurants, striped bass, swordfish, mako shark, tuna, blackfish, cod, and monkfish are local and wild. Salmon, Chilean sea bass, tilapia, catfish, trout and many others are farmed around the world and shipped fresh.

Filet of Sole Meuniere

Yield: 4 portions

Ingredients	Amounts
flounder fillets	2 lb.
salt	1 tbsp.
white pepper	1 tsp.
flour	1 cup
unsalted butter	4 oz.
fresh lemon juice	2 tbsp.
chopped parsley	¼ cup
unsalted butter, cold	2 oz.
slices of peeled lemon	to garnish

Procedure:

1. Season flounder with salt and pepper. Dredge in flour and shake off excess.

2. Heat saute pan (or pans) and add butter. Place fish fillets in pan flesh side down (presentation side). Saute until lightly browned and turn with spatula. Remove from pan and place on hot dinner plates.

3. Heat cold butter in same pan until it begins to brown. Quickly add lemon juice and chopped parsley and pour over fish. Garnish with sliced lemon.

Note: Add ¼ cup of slivered almonds to the pan when adding cold butter and lemon juice to make flounder amandine.

Recommended Wine: Crisp Chardonnay; Sauvignon Blanc; Dry Riesling

Flounder Poached in White Wine Sauce
(Sole Vin Blanc)

Yield: 4 portions

Ingredients	Amounts
flounder fillets	2 lb.
salt	2 tsp.
white pepper	1 tsp.
shallots, finely diced	½ cup
butter	2 oz.
Long Island chardonnay (stainless steel fermented)	1 cup
heavy cream	1 cup
lemon juice	1 tbsp.

Procedure:

1. Season flounder with salt and pepper. Cut fillets down lateral line and roll them into small "paupiettes."
2. Butter shallow baking pan and sprinkle shallots in bottom. Place flounder on top of shallots and pour wine over all.
3. Cover fish with buttered parchment paper or foil. Place in hot 425°F oven and cook until fish is opaque (about 15 min.).
4. Remove from oven and put fish on warm plates. Strain liquid into small saucepan and reduce by two-thirds. Add cream and lemon juice. Check for seasoning and spoon over flounder.

Notes:

1. In classical cookery a fish veloute would be included. Make fish stock from the head and rack and thicken it with roux. Combine this veloute with the cream and lemon juice.
2. If you add one cup of sliced white mushrooms to the shallots in the poaching pan and do not strain liquid, it is called "Sole Bonne Femme."
3. If you add two cups of tomato concasse and ¼ cup chopped parsley to poaching pan and substitute cold butter for the heavy cream, you have "Sole Duglere."
4. If you add two cups of seedless green grapes cut in half to the poaching pan plus ¼ cup chopped parsley, you have "Sole Veronique." This recipe shows how flounder is complimented by many different flavor accents.

Recommended Wine: Stainless Steel Fermented Chardonnay, Dry Riesling, Sauvignon Blanc

Baked Flounder with Shrimp and Oyster Stuffing

Yield: 4 portions

Ingredients	Amounts
flounder fillets	1½ lb.
butter	2 oz.
oysters, shucked	½ pint
shrimp, raw, peeled, deveined	1 cup
scallions, finely chopped	¼ cup
celery, finely chopped	¼ cup
red pepper, finely chopped	¼ cup
fresh thyme, chopped	1 tbsp.
parsley, chopped	2 tbsp.
dry sherry	2 tbsp.
french bread, chopped	about 1 cup
salt and ground black pepper	to taste
paprika	1 tbsp.

Procedure:

1. Melt butter in saute pan and add oysters. Cook until edges curl and remove with slotted spoon. Add shrimp to same pan and cook in oyster juices until opaque. Remove and set aside. Chop shrimp and oysters coarsely and combine.

2. Add scallions, celery, and red pepper to same pan with oyster and shrimp juices. Cook briefly and stir in thyme, parsley, and sherry. Add enough French bread to absorb liquid. Fold in chopped oysters and shrimp. Check for seasoning.

3. Place a spoon of stuffing on flounder fillet and fold in half. Place stuffed fillets on buttered baking pan. Brush a little butter on top and sprinkle with paprika. Season with salt and pepper and bake, uncovered, for about 20 minutes in 400°F oven.

4. Serve over wilted greens such as spinach, arugula, or broccoli rabe. Garnish with lemon.

Recommended Wine: Barrel Fermented Chardonnay

41

Poached Striped Bass with Gewurztraminer

Yield: 4 Portions

Ingredients	Amounts
bass fillets, boneless skinless, 6 oz each	4
shallots, chopped fine	1 cup
olive oil	2 tbsp.
salt	1 tbsp.
pepper	1 tsp.
Gewurztraminer wine	2 cups
ginger, fresh grated	1 tsp.
grapefruit sections	15
mint leaves, chopped	½ cup
fish veloute or cold butter	½ cup

Procedure:

1. Season bass with salt and pepper. Coat large saute pan with oil and shallots. Place fish in pan and pour wine over fish to almost cover.

2. Cover fish with foil and bring to a boil. Simmer until fish is just cooked (about 10 min.) and remove fish to warm place.

3. Reduce cooking liquid by half and add ginger and grapefruit. Stir in cold butter or fish veloute. Add fish and garnish with mint leaves.

Notes: Bass is sold whole or with the head and racks. Make fish stock by cooking head and bones in water with onions, celery, bay leaf, thyme and peppercorns. Cook for only 30 minutes. Strain and cool. Thicken this with roux and season with salt and pepper to make veloute.

Recommended Wine: Long Island Gewurztraminer

Roasted Blackfish with Potato Crust

Yield: 8 portions

Ingredients	Amounts

blackfish fillets
  boneless, skinless, cut in
    4 oz. pieces about ½" thick
	2 lbs.

olive oil	¼ cup
Aioli sauce (recipe, next page)	1 cup
Yukon gold potatoes	2 lbs.
grated Parmesan cheese	½ cup
chef's salt (see p. 34)	2 tbsp.
paprika	1 tbsp.

Procedure:

1. Brush oil on a sheet pan and place blackfish on the pan about one inch apart. Season with chef's salt.

2. Boil potatoes in their skins until just cooked. Cool under cold water and peel. Grate with a hand grater on the coarse side.

3. Spread Aioli sauce on fish about ⅛" thick. Sprinkle shredded potatoes over top and sides of fish. Do not pack down.

4. Sprinkle Parmesan cheese, paprika and chef's salt over potatoes.

5. Roast in a preheated 425°F oven until potatoes are brown (about 15 minutes).

6. Serve over wilted greens such as broccoli rabe, spinach or arugula.

Notes: This same recipe is very good with swordfish or cod. For easy assembly cook potatoes the day before and chill. Make Aioli sauce ahead also.

Recommended Wine: A crisp Chardonnay.

Aioli Sauce

Yield: 1 cup

Ingredients	Amounts
bread crumbs	1 tbsp.
wine vinegar	1 tbsp.
garlic, minced	4 cloves
egg yolks	2
olive oil	¾ cup
salt	½ tsp.
cayenne pepper	pinch
lemon juice	1 tbsp.

Procedure:

1. Chop the garlic as fine as possible and mix with the vinegar and bread crumbs in a mixing bowl. Stir in egg yolks.

2. With a whisk, beat in olive oil, starting just a few drops at a time and gradually increasing the amount until it looks like mayonnaise.

3. Season with salt, cayenne, and lemon juice.

Note: For a faster substitute, you can simply mix finely minced garlic with commercial mayonnaise. Add a little lemon juice and cayenne. If you have a mortar and pestle, use it to mash the garlic.

Swordfish Piccata

Yield: 4 portions

Ingredients	Amounts
swordfish, cut fresh in a single block	1½ lbs.
lemons	2
chef's salt	to taste
eggs	2
grated Parmesan cheese	¼ cup
flour	½ cup
milk	¼ cup
olive oil	¼ cup
capers	¼ cup
butter, cold	2 tbsp.
chopped parsley	2 tbsp.

Procedure:

1. Trim skin and excess fat off fish. Cut across the grain into ¼" thick slices. Sprinkle with chef's salt.
2. Remove zest from one lemon with a sharp paring knife. Cut into little julienne pieces and set aside. Peel lemon and cut into thin slices. Reserve.
3. Make a batter by whisking together the eggs, Parmesan cheese, half the flour, and milk.
4. Heat the olive oil in a large saute pan over medium heat. Dust the fish in flour and dip it into the batter. Panfry fish in hot oil until golden brown on each side. Remove. Pour off excess oil.
5. Stir the juice from the second lemon into the saute pan, stirring to deglaze. Swirl in cold butter and chopped parsley. Add capers and lemon slices. Pour over fish.

Notes: This dish is spectacular when served over homemade Fettucine (see recipe p. 36). It is also good served over Linguine.

Personal Note: When my daughter was little she announced that she didn't eat seafood. So I served her this dish and told her that it was a local breed of turkey called "aquaturkey."

Recommended Wine: Barrel Fermented Chardonnay

Cornmeal Blini with Smoked Salmon

Yield: 12 Appetizer Portions

Ingredients	Amounts
flour, all purpose	1 cup
cornmeal	1 cup
baking powder	4 tsp.
salt	1 tsp.
milk	2 cups
eggs	2
melted butter	¼ cup
smoked salmon, sliced	1 lb.
sour cream	1 cup
chives	2 tbsp.
capers, or salmon caviar	2 tbsp.

Procedure:

1. Combine flour, cornmeal, baking powder and salt in a bowl.

2. In a separate bowl beat milk and eggs together.

3. Pour milk and eggs into flour mixture and stir in melted butter.

4. Heat a six-inch no-stick saute pan (or spray regular pan with no-stick) and ladle in 2 tbsp. batter. Cook until bubbly and flip over. Cook one minute and remove.

5. Place salmon slices on blini and garnish with sour cream, chives, capers or caviar.

Note: During corn season serve this dish with corn salsa (see recipe, next page).

Recommended Wine: Sauvignon Blanc or Gewurztraminer

Corn Salsa

Yield: 8 Portions

Ingredients	Amounts
extra virgin olive oil	½ cup
lemon juice	2 tbsp.
red wine vinegar	3 tbsp.
garlic, minced	2 tbsp.
Tabasco sauce	1 tsp.
fresh corn on the cob, uncooked	6 ears
tomatoes, peeled, seeded, chopped	2 cups
red pepper, diced	½ cup
yellow pepper, diced	½ cup
jalapeño peppers, minced	2
onion, finely diced	1 cup
tarragon, chopped	1 tbsp.
parsley, chopped	2 tbsp.
basil, chopped	2 tbsp.
ground black pepper	1 tsp.
salt	2 tsp.

Procedure:

1. Shuck corn and remove kernels with a sharp paring knife.
2. Whisk together oil lemon juice, vinegar, and garlic.
3. Mix all ingredients in a bowl and chill.

Tomato Salsa

Yield: 8 Portions

Ingredients	Amounts
tomatoes, peeled, seeded, chopped	6
scallions, chopped finely	6
garlic, minced	1 tbsp.
cilantro, chopped	2 tbsp.
jalapeño peppers, minced	2
lemon juice	2 tbsp.
ground cumin	1 tsp.
salt	2 tsp.
pepper	1 tsp.

Combine all ingredients in a bowl, mix together and chill.

47

Monkfish Stew

Yield: 4 portions

Ingredients	Amounts
monkfish fillets, boned, skinned and cut into 1" chunks	2 lbs.
olive oil	½ cup
flour	1 cup
salt	1 tsp.
pepper	1 tsp.
mushrooms, quartered	2 cups
garlic, minced	1 tbsp.
chicken broth	1 cup
white wine	1 cup
saffron, dissolved in a little chicken broth	½ tsp.
sugar snap peas	2 cups
pitted black or green olives	½ cup
pimiento, cut in squares	½ cup
new potatoes, peeled, bite sized, cooked	1½ lbs.
chopped parsley	¼ cup

Procedure:

1. Dredge monkfish in seasoned flour and brown at high heat in olive oil. Remove.

2. Add mushrooms and garlic to pan and saute. Deglaze with wine and add chicken broth and saffron. Taste for seasoning.

3. Add back monkfish and simmer until just cooked (about 5 min.). Add peas, cooked new potatoes, olives and pimiento. Bring to a boil, add chopped parsley and serve.

Recommended Wine: Voignier or Dry Riesling.

Cedar Planked Arctic Char
with Duchess Potatoes and Asparagus

Yield: 4 portions

Ingredients	Amounts
Cedar roofing shingles	four 4"x6" shingles, soaked in water
olive oil	¼ cup
Arctic char fillets, skinless boneless	four 8 oz. fillets
Dijon mustard	2 tbsp.
Japanese bread crumbs (panko)	1 cup
chef's salt	1 tbsp.
paprika	1 tsp.
Yukon Gold potatoes	2 lbs.
butter	2 tbsp.
egg	1
salt	1 tsp.
white pepper	½ tsp.
asparagus	2 lbs.

Procedure:

1. Place shingles on sheet pan. Brush with oil. Place fish on shingles and coat with mustard. Sprinkle bread crumbs, paprika and chef's salt over fish.

2. Peel potatoes, cut in chunks and boil until tender. Mash and add egg, butter and seasoning. Place in pastry bag with large star tube and pipe around edge of fish.

3. Coat asparagus with oil, season, and place around fish.

4. Put fish in 425°F oven and cook until fish flakes easily (about 15 minutes).

Notes: This entire recipe also cooks very well in a covered outdoor char grill. Shingles can be purchased at a lumber yard or home store. You can substitute salmon for arctic char.

Recommended Wine: Barrel Fermented Chardonnay

White Fish Stew

Yield: 10 portions

Ingredients	Amounts
striped bass	1 whole fish
cod fillet	1 lb.
monkfish fillet	1 lb.
halibut fillet	1 lb.
onion, sliced thin	2 cups
fennel, sliced	1 cup
leeks, white part	1 cup
parsley stems	6
bay leaf	1
salt	1 tbsp.
white wine	2 cups
fish stock	2 cups
new potatoes, peeled, small	12
pearl onions, peeled	1 cup
white mushrooms, quartered	2 cup
baby carrots	2 cup
parsnips, peeled, cut on bias	1 cup
egg yolks	4
aioli sauce (see recipe p. 44)	2 cups
parsley, chopped	½ cup

Procedure:

1. Fillet striped bass and make stock from head and rack. Skin fillets and cut into 2" chunks. Repeat with other fish.

2. Place fish in a sautoir and add onion, fennel, leeks, parsley stems, bay leaf and salt. Cover with wine and fish stock. Cook until fish is just done (about 15 min.). Set fish aside. Strain broth into another pan. Cook potatoes, onions, mushrooms, carrots, and parsnips in broth until tender. (If desired, omit straining broth.)

3. Blend egg yolks and aioli sauce together and add to broth. Bring up to simmer — do not boil. Add fish, check for seasoning and sprinkle with parsley.

Recommended Wine: Riesling, Viognier

Broiled Cod with Cod Cakes
Yield: 8 portions

Ingredients	Amounts
cod fillets, boneless, skinless	3 lbs.
melted butter	½ cup
chef's salt	2 tbsp.
paprika	1 tbsp.

Procedure:

1. Purchase a whole side of cod. Trim out thin line of bones. Cut center into eight 6 oz. portions. Place them on a broiler pan, and coat with melted butter. Sprinkle with paprika and chef's salt. Broil until fish turns opaque — about 10 minutes.
2. Cut cod trimmings into chunks. Check for bones and boil cod for 3 minutes in salted water. Drain and cool.

Cod Cakes

Ingredients	Amounts	
cooked cod	1 lb. (about 2 cups)	
mashed potatoes, unsalted, fresh	2 cups	
whole egg	1	
egg yolk	1	
salt	2 tsp.	
white pepper	1 tsp.	
ground ginger	¼ tsp.	
flour	1 cup	⎫
egg wash (one egg mixed with one cup milk)		⎬ breading
bread crumbs	1 cup	⎭
olive oil	¼ cup	

Procedure:
1. Flake cooked cod into a bowl. Add mashed potatoes, whole egg, egg yolk, and seasoning. Mix with a spoon.
2. Using an ice cream scoop, divide mixture into 8 portions. Dredge in flour, dip in egg wash, and roll in bread crumbs.
3. Flatten cod cakes into rounds and saute in olive oil until golden brown. Put on plate beside broiled fish and garnish with lemon tartar sauce.

Recommended Wine: Stainless Steel Fermented Chardonnay; Sauvignon Blanc

Tuna Steak Au Poivre

Yield: 4 portions

Ingredients	Amounts
tuna steaks, ¾" thick	4 (about 2 lbs.)
black peppercorns	¼ cup
olive oil	2 tbsp.
brandy	¼ cup
heavy cream	1 cup
Dijon mustard	1 tbsp.

Procedure:

1. Place peppercorns on cutting board and crush them with the bottom of a small saute pan. Press down on peppercorns and roll pan (if you have a mortar and pestle it works well.) The peppercorns should be cracked but not too finely crushed. Press them into both sides of tuna steaks.

2. Heat heavy cast iron skillet very hot and add a little oil. Cook tuna steaks at high heat until crusty on outside but still rare in the middle. Do not crowd steaks; cook in batches if necessary.

3. Remove steaks from heat and add brandy. Hold pan near open flame or touch with match to ignite. (Be careful.) Remove steaks to warm plate and deglaze pan with cream. Stir in mustard and pour over tuna.

Recommended Wine: Peppercorns leave a hot taste which is not wine friendly. A full bodied beer might be best with this recipe.

Note: Simply grilled tuna is very good with merlot.

**Long Island
Duck**

How Did the Long Island Duck Become Famous?

Ducks have been farmed on Long island since the late 1600's. In the early days all duck production was part of mixed farming. The sandy soil, easy access to water for ponds and a good market in New York City made Long Island a natural for specialization. In 1868, the Long Island Railroad was completed as far out as Eastport. Eastport soon became the center of our local duck industry.

Two of the earliest duck farms were the Atlantic, founded by Warren Hallock in 1858, and the Oceanic, founded in 1883. They were both located in Speonk. The Oceanic stayed in business for 90 years, making it the oldest duck farm in America. But the event that made the Long Island Duck world famous began with the introduction of the Pekin Duck from China in 1873. This large-framed breed thrived in our region, producing big portions of very tender meat. The Long Island Duck joined the Rouen duck in France and the Pekin duck in China to become the world's most sought-after ducks.

How did those first Pekin ducks get to Long Island? According to Lloyd Corwin, owner of Crescent Duck Farm, a British officer named Ashley, stationed in Peking cultivated a few white ducks of uncommon size for his private consumption. In 1873, an American clipper ship came to Peking from Connecticut, carrying a Yankee trader named James Palmer. Palmer returned to the United States with a small flock of Ashley's ducks. One drake and three female ducks survived the trip, and their descendants grew rapidly on the sandy soil and tide-water streams of Eastern Long Island.

By 1897, about 200,000 ducks were produced annually by all the duck farms. By 1922, production had grown to two million, and in 1968 six million ducks were produced by about thirty growers. Today this number has dropped to about two million, with only two major producers left — Crescent Duck Farm of Aquebogue and Jurgielewicz Duck Farm of Moriches. Both of these operations work out of modern state-of-the-art facilities and continue the tradition of quality that Long Island is famous for.

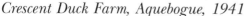

Crescent Duck Farm, Aquebogue, 1941

Roast Crisp Long Island Duck with Plum Sauce

Yield: 4 Portions

Ingredients

6 lb. Long Island Duck
onion, quartered
chef's salt
honey
butcher's twine or string

Procedure:

1. Remove giblets and neck from duck cavity and rinse under cold water.

2. Cut off tail, flap of neck skin and wing tips.

3. Place onion and chef's salt into cavity.

4. Push legs up against breasts and tie with butcher's twine. Tie wings against body.

5. Puncture the duck skin with a fork, brush lightly with honey and season with chef's salt.

6. Place duck on its side, on a rack in a shallow pan. Cook in pre-heated 500°F oven about 20 minutes. Turn duck onto other side and repeat. It should be lightly browned.

7. Reduce oven heat to 425° F and place duck breast side up. Cover loosely with foil and cook for 1½ hours. The duck will be very crisp and brown as the honey carmelizes.

8. Remove and cool at room temperature. Split in half with a chef's knife and remove backbone. Using fingers, remove rib bones and cartilage. Twist out thigh bone. Reheat duck briefly in hot oven just before serving.

9. Make plum sauce (recipe, next page). Garnish with dried apricots, raisins, prunes and beach plums if available.

Note: Serve duck with long grain wild rice, and braised red cabbage (recipe, p. 90).

Recommended Wine: Merlot

Wild Beach Plum Sauce for Ducks
Yield: 1 quart

Ingredients	Amounts
duck stock (or chicken broth)*	1 quart
red wine vinegar	1 cup
brown sugar	1 cup
whole orange, quartered	1
whole lemon, quarted	1
cinnamon sticks	2
whole cloves	6
black peppercorns	1 tsp.
salt	as needed
cornstarch/cold water	¼ cup each
wild beach plum jam	½ cup
plums, pitted and cut in half for garnish	12

Procedure:

1. In a small heavy saucepan, cook brown sugar at medium heat until it begins to caramelize. Carefully stir with fork until it is dark brown and liquid. Add vinegar and let it boil until it becomes syrup (about 20 minutes).

2. In a separate saucepan, heat duck stock and thicken lightly with cornstarch/water solution. Squeeze cut oranges and lemons into stock and add rinds to stock. Add cinnamon sticks, cloves and black pepper. Simmer ½ hour.

3. Add carmelized sugar/vinegar to stock along with beach plum jam (you can substitute currant jelly). Check for seasoning and strain. Garnish with plums and serve over duck quarters.

*To make simple duck stock, brown duck neck, wing tips and giblets (except liver) on top of stove in a little oil with chunks of carrot, celery, and onion. Place in saucepan with a quart of canned chicken broth and cook for 1½ hours. Strain and cool, skim fat and use in recipe.

Roasted Duck Cakes

Yield: 12 cakes (about 12 appetizer portions)

Ingredients	Amounts
cooked duck meat skinless, boneless	1½ lbs. (about 3 cups)
bread crumbs, dry, unseasoned	½ cup
mayonnaise	½ cup
eggs, beaten	2
Dijon mustard	1 tbsp.
Worcestershire sauce	1 tbsp.
cayenne pepper	½ tsp.
thyme	1 tsp.
red pepper, finely diced	½ cup
green pepper, finely diced	½ cup
toasted almonds, chopped	¼ cup
salt	2 tsp.
pepper	1 tsp.
scallion, chopped fine	½ cup
parsley, chopped fine	¼ cup
Japanese bread crumbs (panko)	2 cups

Note: Leftover roast duck is the easiest source for duck meat. If you don't have that, roast a five pound duck in the oven at 400° F for about 1½ hours. This recipe is also very good using smoked duck. Serve the duck cakes with plum sauce (recipe, p. 57) or garnish them with dried apricots, prunes, raisins or cranberries.

Procedure:

1. Chop duck meat finely with a chef's knife.

2. Mix all other ingredients in bowl, except Japanese bread crumbs. Add duck and stir together.

3. Form into 2 oz. balls and roll in Japanese bread crumbs. Flatten into cakes and place on lightly oiled sheet pan.

4. Roast in 400°F oven for ten minutes. Turn with spatula and cook another five minutes (they should be golden brown).

Note: For small quantities, saute in oil or butter instead of heating in oven.

Ragout of Duck Merlot

Yield: 4 portions

Ingredients	Amounts
duck breasts, skin on	8
flour, seasoned with salt and pepper	1 cup
shallots, cut in chunks	2 cups
garlic, minced	2 tbsp
carrots, cut on bias, one inch	2 cups
mushrooms, quartered	2 cups
flour	¼ cup
Merlot	1 cup
chicken broth	2 cups
parsley	¼ cup

Procedure:

1. Remove skin from duck. Reserve. Cut duck breasts into one inch chunks. Cut skin and fat into squares.

2. In heavy sauce pan or brazier brown duck skin, rendering fat. Remove crisp skin and set aside. Discard most of fat. Toss duck meat in seasoned flour.

3. At high heat, brown duck meat in remaining duck fat. Remove and set aside. Add shallots, garlic, carrots, and mushrooms. Saute at medium heat until lightly browned. Stir in flour and brown. Stir in merlot and chicken broth and bring to a boil. Add duck meat, and bring to a boil.

4. Add crisp duck skin (chopped into small pieces) and parsley. Serve over egg noodles, wild rice, or barley.

Note: A whole duck is excellent for this recipe. Bone it completely, reserving skin, and make stock with the bones and carcass. Substitute stock for chicken broth in recipe.

Recommended Wine: Merlot

Pan Seared Duck Breast with Cranberries and Roasted Duck Legs

Yield: 4 portions

Ingredients	Amounts
5 lb. Long Island ducks	2
onions, coarsely chopped	2 cups
carrots, coarsely chopped	2 cups
celery, coarsely chopped	2 cups
leek, white part, chopped	1
parsley stems ⎫	6
bay leaf ⎪ tie in	2
peppercorns ⎬ cheese- cloth	10
thyme ⎪ bag	1 tsp.
garlic ⎭	2 cloves
sugar	¼ cup
cranberries	2 cups
butter	2 tbsp
shallots	½ cup
reduced duck stock	1 cup
chef's salt	to taste
honey	¼ cup
orange juice	¼ cup
soy sauce	2 tbsp.

Procedure:

1. Rinse ducks, remove giblets and neck from cavity, and bone out breasts. Remove leg and thigh sections at thigh joint and set aside. Place duck carcasses with necks in roasting pan and cook at 400°F for about 45 min. Add onions, carrots, celery, and leek and cook 15 min. more.

2. Transfer roasted bones and vegetables to a stock pot. Pour off fat from roast pan and deglaze with water. Add this to stock pot along with water to cover bones. Bring to a boil and skim the surface. Reduce heat to simmer, add

cheesecloth "Bouquet Garni" and cook for 3 hours. Strain and cool overnight.

3. Place duck legs and thighs in pan with honey, orange juice, and soy sauce and refrigerate overnight.

4. Remove stock from refrigerator and discard fat which has risen to surface. Place stock in saucepan and reduce by two-thirds. Season with salt and pepper.

5. Cook cranberries with sugar and a little water until skins pop. Drain cranberries and set aside.

6. Place duck legs in roasting pan and brush with a little honey. Season with chef's salt. Roast, uncovered in 400° oven for one hour or until very crisp.

7. In saute pan sear duck breasts at high heat with the skin side down. Turn and cook briefly on the other side and remove. Pour off excess fat and add butter and shallots. Add one cup of reduced duck stock and cranberries. Bring to a boil and check for seasoning.

8 Remove skin from duck breast if desired and slice. It should be medium rare.

9. Place duck legs on plate with sliced duck breast. Strain sauce into bowl and spoon onto plate.

Note: Serve with braised red cabbage (recipe, p. 90) and potato pancakes (recipe, p. 88).

Recommended Wine: Long Island Merlot.

Cannelloni of Fresh Greens and Duck

Yield: 4 portions

Ingredients	Amounts
olive oil	2 tbsp.
spinach, stems removed	4 cups
arugula, stems removed	4 cups
leaf lettuce, coarsely chopped	4 cups
parsley, chopped	½ cup
tarragon	1 tbsp.
cooked duck meat, skinless, boneless, julienne strips	2 cups (about 1 lb.)
chef's salt	1 tbsp
fresh egg pasta (recipe p. 36)	8 oz. cut into 8 rectangles very thin, 3" x 4"
Parmesan cheese	½ cup
duck stock (or chicken broth)	2 cups
Parmesan cheese	¼ cup

Procedure:

1. Heat oil in large saute pan. Add spinach, arugula, lettuce, parsley, and tarragon. Cook until wilted (2 min). Drain into colander, cool, and chop.

2. Mix julienned duck meat with wilted greens and season with chef's salt.

3. Cook pasta rectangles in boiling, salted water until tender. Drain, rinse, and cool.

4. Lay out pasta on cutting board, sprinkle with grated parmesan and place duck mixture in middle. Roll up pasta into cylinders (cannelloni) and place in oiled baking pan.

5. Add stock to half cover cannelloni. Sprinkle with cheese and put in 350° oven for 20 minutes. Serve over excess greens or additional spinach.

Notes: Boneless, skinless duck breasts can be used. Saute them in a little oil until medium rare. Cut into strips for recipe. Commercial lasagna can be substituted for home-made pasta.

Recommended Wine: Cabernet Franc

Boneless Roast Duck Legs
with apple, walnut, apricot stuffing and barley pilaf

Yield: 4 portions

Ingredients	Amounts
duck legs (includes leg and thigh)	8
barley	1 cup
salt	1 tsp.
shallots, chopped	½ cup
apples, peeled, cored, diced	1 cup
butter	2 tbsp.
dried apricots, chopped	½ cup
pitted prunes, chopped	½ cup
walnuts, chopped	1 cup
apricot brandy	¼ cup
salt	1 tsp.
pepper	1 tsp.
honey/brandy glaze	¼ cup

Procedure:

1. Bone duck legs by making an incision along the underside right against the leg bone and thigh bone. Expose the bones, cut around the joint and remove bones. Leave skin intact.

2. Cook barley until tender in salted boiling water (about 20 mins.).

3. Saute shallots and apples in butter. Add apricots, prunes, and walnuts. Season with salt, pepper, and brandy. Combine with barley.

4. Mix ¼ cup of honey with 1 tsp. of brandy for glaze.

5. Place a small spoon of this stuffing into each duck leg. Roll up duck leg and secure with a tooth pick. Place duck legs in shallow roasting pan and brush with glaze. Roast at 350°F for one hour. Save excess stuffing to serve on the side.

Note: For a simpler version of this recipe, do not bone the duck legs. Paint them with glaze, season, and roast for one hour at 400°F. Serve barley stuffing on the side.

Recommended Wine: Merlot

Chargrilled Breast of Duck with Orecchiette Pasta

Yield: 4 portions

Ingredients	Amounts
duck breast, boneless, skinless	2 lb.
portabello mushrooms	4
green pepper, split in half, cleaned	2
red pepper, split in half, cleaned	2
Spanish onion, peeled, cut in thick slices	1
sun dried tomato, cut in pieces	½ cup
garlic, minced	1 tbsp.
orecchiette pasta	1 lb.
extra virgin olive oil	½ cup
balsamic vinegar	¼ cup
fresh basil, chopped	½ cup
ground black pepper	2 tsp.
coarse salt	1 tbsp.
Italian flat leaf parsley, chopped	½ cup
Tabasco sauce	1 tsp.
Parmesan cheese	to garnish

Procedure:

1. Brush duck breast with oil, season with coarse salt and black pepper, and grill over live charcoal. Cook brown on outside and rare in the middle, about 5 minutes.

2. Char-grill peppers and onion. Do not completely blacken peppers; leave them a little undercooked. Remove and scrape any burnt skin off. Dice peppers and onion into large chunks.

3. Cook pasta in boiling water until al dente, and drain.

4. Cut duck breast into bite sized chunks.

5. Char-grill portabello mushroom caps until just done (5 min.), and cut into 1" chunks.

6. Combine all ingredients in large bowl and toss together. Serve warm with grated Parmesan cheese.

Recommended Wine: Cabernet Franc; Pinot Noir

Meat and Poultry

Pecan Chicken

Yield: 4 Portions

Ingredients	Amounts
boneless, skinless chicken breasts cut about ¼" thick	1½ lbs.
chef's salt	1 tbsp.
butter	1 cup
Dijon mustard	2 tbsp.
pecan pieces	1 cup
bread crumbs	1 cup
olive oil	¼ cup
sour cream	1 cup
Dijon mustard	1 tbsp.

Procedure:

1. Melt butter and combine it with mustard in a bowl.

2. Chop pecans finely and combine with bread crumbs in a flat pan.

3. Season chicken with chef's salt.

3. Dredge chicken in butter mixture and place in pecan mixture. Pound crumbs into chicken with your hands.

4. Heat oil in saute pan and cook chicken at medium heat until golden brown, turn, and saute until fully cooked (10 min.).

5. Remove chicken, pour off any excess oil, and add sour cream and mustard to pan. Stir and pour over chicken.

Recommended Wine: Barrel Fermented Chardonnay

Roast Chicken

Yield: 4 portions

Ingredients	Amounts
whole chicken	3½ lbs.
chef's salt	1 tsp.
butter, softened	1 tbsp.
mirepoix:	
onions, diced ¼"	1 cup
carrots, diced ¼"	½ cup
celery, diced ¼"	½ cup
lemon pepper seasoning	1 tsp.
chicken broth	2 cups
flour	½ cup
string or butcher's twine	

Procedure:

1. Remove giblets from chicken. Remove excess fat and rinse cavity.

2. Season cavity with chef's salt.

3. Truss chicken with string or twine (fold wings behind back and tie string around them; push legs down under breast meat and tie a string around them).

4. Dice vegetables for mirepoix and put them in bottom of small roasting pan. Place chicken on top of mirepoix and rub soft butter on chicken. Sprinkle lemon pepper seasoning over chicken.

5. Roast chicken uncovered in 325°F oven about 1 hour and 15 min. or until internal temperature reads 170°F. Baste chicken 2 or 3 times.

6. Remove chicken and place on serving platter. Add flour to pan drippings and place on stove until lightly brown. Stir in chicken broth and bring to a boil. Strain sauce into sauce pan and adjust seasoning.

Recommended Wine: Stainless Steel Fermented Chardonnay

Fried Chicken

Yield: 4 portions

Ingredients	Amounts
whole chicken, cut in 8 pieces	3 lbs.
chef's salt	
Batter:	
egg	1
milk	1 cup
flour	¾ cup
Breading mixture:	
salt	1 tbsp.
pepper	1 tsp.
flour	1 cup
Japanese bread crumbs (panko)	1 cup
oil for deep frying or pan frying	

Procedure:

1. With a boning knife, cut chicken in 8 pieces. (Remove wings first, then thigh/leg, then cut along backbone, notch breast bone and remove, then cut breast into two.)

2. Place pieces skin side up on sheet pan, sprinkle with chefs salt, and roast in 350° oven for hour. Chicken will be fully cooked. Save drippings for gravy. Remove chicken and refrigerate.

3. Make batter in a bowl. Combine breading mixture in shallow pan. Heat oil to 350° for deep frying.

4. Dip chicken pieces in batter and roll in breading mixture. Press crumbs onto chicken with your hands.

5. Cook in deep fryer until golden brown, about 5 minutes. (You can pan fry chicken in a cast iron skillet. Heat ¼" of oil over medium heat. Add chicken and turn once.)

Note: This recipe can be prepared a day or two ahead. When you roast the chicken first it throws off a lot of fat, making the final product very crispy. If desired you can purchase chicken parts instead of cutting it yourself.

Chicken Croquettes

Yield: 12 portions

Ingredients	Amounts
butter	4 oz.
onion, finely chopped	1 cup
celery, finely chopped	½ cup
red pepper, finely chopped	¼ cup
green pepper, finely chopped	¼ cup
flour	½ cup
chicken stock	2 cups
cooked chicken meat, skinless, boneless, chopped finely	1½ lbs.
salt	1 tbsp.
white pepper	2 tsp.
nutmeg	1 tsp.
egg, beaten	1
parsley, chopped	½ cup

Procedure:

1. Melt butter in large saute pan and add onion, celery, and peppers. Cook on low heat until vegetables are just cooked.
2. Stir in flour to make roux. Cook at low heat for 5 minutes. Add chicken stock and stir. Bring slowly to a boil. Mixture should be very thick.
3. Add chicken meat, salt, pepper, nutmeg, egg, and parsley. Simmer until all ingredients are hot but not boiling. Transfer to a shallow pan and refrigerate.

Breading: Put 2 cups of flour in a shallow pan. Season with salt and pepper. Break one egg into a bowl and add one cup of milk. Stir. Place 2 cups of plain bread crumbs in a shallow pan. Using a scoop, scoop chilled croquette mixture from pan and place in flour. Dip in egg wash and roll in crumbs. Set on a tray and form into a croquette with fingers. Chill.

Cooking: Deep fry at 350°F until golden brown, about 5 minutes. Serve with chicken gravy or cream sauce or place them on a bed of greens with lemon.

Note: You can also roast croquettes in the oven instead of deep-frying; cook at 350°F for 20 minutes.

Steaks

Outdoor grilling is immensely popular on the North Fork and everyone loves the tantalizing aromas and the almost religious rituals that surround the meal.

Beef:

Beef steaks come in two important categories: tender and less tender. The tender steaks are expensive depending on grade and type of aging. In general, they should be simply cooked with a minimum of seasoning.

New York strip steak is the most popular of all steaks. The largest percentage are graded USDA Choice. Branded steaks such as Black Angus and Hereford are not graded but usually of very high quality. A very small amount of beef is graded USDA Prime. It is very tender with extensive marbling and a high fat content. Dry aged beef is the most tender and flavorful. It must be aged for up to three weeks in carcass form under controlled conditions of temperature and humidity.

Seasoning Steak and Preparing it for the Grill:

Brush a little oil on the steaks and clean the grill. Build a fire with charcoal and allow the coals to turn white. Season meat with Kosher salt and cracked black pepper. Place steaks on hot grill at 45° angle. After two minutes, turn to opposite 45° angle from grill. This will result in beautiful cross hatching. After two more minutes turn steaks and cover with lid. Rare steaks take about five minutes. For exact doneness, use an instant read meat thermometer. Medium rare should read 120°F.

The Rib Steak and Filet Mignon are the other two popular tender steaks. Cook them the same as strip steak.

The Less Tender Beef Steaks:

These steaks lend themselves to more creative marinades, seasonings and accompaniments. It is essential to cook them rare or medium rare to avoid a tough, chewy result.

The Flank Steak:

Prepare a marinade by combining one cup of olive oil, one tablespoon chopped garlic, one tablespoon chopped fresh rosemary, 2 bay leaves, and two tablespoons chopped shallots. Stir in ¼ cup lemon juice, a teaspoon Kosher salt and a teaspoon of cracked black pepper. Pour over flank steak in shallow pan or sealable plastic bag. Refrigerate one hour or more. Boil new potatoes in their skins until just tender. Place them in marinade if desired. Dry meat with paper towel and place on grill. Skewer potatoes with metal skewer and cook alongside of meat. Cut meat across grain into thin slices.

Bourbon Steak and Omaha Hash Browns:

This recipe is very good with a boneless top butt sirloin steak. Use a cast iron skillet to pan sear it. Season steak with Kosher salt and cracked black pepper. Place in a shallow pan and sprinkle with ½ cup of chopped shallots. Combine one tablespoon of Dijon mustard with ½ cup of Bourbon and pour over steak. Refrigerate one hour. Meanwhile, boil two pounds of Idaho potatoes in their skins until tender. Cool under cold water. Peel and shred with a box grater. At service time, remove steaks and dry with paper towels. Heat skillet very hot. Cook steaks about five minutes on each side and remove pan from heat. Pour marinade over steak and ignite with match to flame. Remove steak to warm place and swirl 2 tablespoons of unsalted butter into pan. Pour sauce over steaks. For potatoes, spray no-stick on saute pan and heat. Add a tablespoon of butter and let it foam. Sprinkle shredded potatoes in pan loosely and season with Kosher salt and pepper. Cook until crispy brown and turn with a rubber spatula. Brown and serve with steak.

Skewered Skirt Steak:

Buy 1½ pounds of skirt steak and cut it into 4 equal pieces. Place meat in a shallow pan and add ½ cup Merlot, 2 tablespoons of olive oil, and 1 tablespoon lemon juice. Add 6 sprigs of fresh rosemary and two bell peppers which have been cut into 3-inch rectangles. Marinate for one hour or more. Weave meat onto a metal skewer with peppers. Tuck rosemary between meat and peppers. Cook on charcoal. Turn once and paint with reserved marinade. Season with Kosher salt and cracked black pepper.

Boneless Roast Turkey Breast

Yield: 8 Portions

Ingredients	Amounts
boneless turkey breast, raw with skin on	about 6 lbs.
Prosciutto ham, diced	1 cup
garlic, minced	1 tbsp.
Fontina cheese, diced	1 cup
fresh parsley, chopped	¼ cup
chef's salt	1 tbsp.
butter	2 oz.
lemon pepper seasoning	1 tbsp.
butcher's twine	as needed

Procedure:

1. If available, buy boneless turkey breast. Or buy a bone-in turkey breast and, using a boning knife, cut along breast bone and rib cage to remove meat. Leave skin on.

2. Butterfly turkey breast by making a horizontal slit along length of meat. Open it up and season with chef's salt.

3. Mix ham, garlic, cheese, and parsley in a bowl. They should be finely diced. Spread stuffing along the cut turkey breast.

4. Roll up turkey breast and tie with butcher's twine. Place in roasting pan and season with lemon pepper seasoning. Cut thin slices of butter and place on top of turkey.

5. Roast, uncovered, in 300°F oven until golden brown. Internal temperature should read 170°F. It should take about 1½ hours.

Notes: You can surround the turkey in the roasting pan with vegetables such as carrots, parsnips, turnips, leeks, and potatoes. Cut them in large chunks and turn them during cooking.

Recommended Wine: Barrel Fermented Chardonnay

Cranberry Chutney

Ingredients	Amounts
fresh cranberries	3 cups
golden raisins	1 cup
sugar	1½ cups
cinnamon, ground	1 tbsp.
ginger, ground	1 tsp.
cloves, ground	½ tsp.
water	½ cup
onion, chopped	½ cup
apple, peeled, cored, chopped	1 cup
celery, diced	½ cup
walnuts, chopped	½ cup

Procedure:

1. Combine cranberries, raisins, sugar, cinnamon, ginger, cloves and water in a saucepan. Cook about 15 minutes or until berries pop and mixture thickens.

2. Stir in onion, apple, celery and walnuts. Simmer 15 minutes. Refrigerate.

Note: This fall condiment goes well with turkey, chicken and duck.

73

Bourbon Glazed Smoked Ham
with Pineapple Raisin Sauce

Yield: 12 Portions

Ingredients	Amounts
boneless smoked ham, fully cooked	10 lbs.
Dijon mustard	¼ cup
bourbon	¼ cup
brown sugar	1 cup
orange juice	¼ cup

Procedure:

1. Mix mustard, bourbon, and brown sugar in bowl. Paint coating on ham with brush.

2. Put ham in 225°F oven in roasting pan and cook, uncovered, until internal temperature reaches 165°F. Continue to baste and paint with glaze.

Notes: If you have a smoker, cook the ham over hickory at low temperature. Indirect cooking in an outdoor char grill is excellent.

See recipe for Pineapple Raisin Sauce on next page.

Recommended Wine: Merlot or Pinot Noir.

Pineapple Raisin Sauce

Yield: One quart

Ingredients	Amounts
brown sugar	½ cup
granulated sugar	½ cup
salt	1 tsp.
ground cloves	½ tsp.
ground cinnamon	1 tsp.
dry mustard	1 tbsp.
corn starch	¼ cup
red wine vinegar	2 tbsp.
beef broth	2 cups
pineapple juice	¼ cup
pineapple chunks	½ cup
raisins	½ cup

Procedure:

1. Mix together all dry ingredients.

2. Heat beef broth to boiling.

3. Add vinegar and pineapple juice to dry ingredients. Stir and add to beef broth.

4. Add pineapple chunks and raisins to sauce.

Goulash

Yield: 4 Portions

Goulash is actually a Hungarian beef soup named after the keepers of Magyar oxen (Gulyas). These recipes were adapted from old recipes by Craig Claiborne, James Beard, and Joseph Wechsberg. I have included them because of the important eastern European presence on the North Fork — and because they are delicious.

Prague Goulash

Ingredients	Amounts
olive oil	2 tbsp.
sliced onions	4 cups
beef stew meat	1 lb.
chef's salt	1 tbsp.
tomato paste	½ cup
veal cubes	8 oz.
pork cubes	8 oz.
white wine	1 cup
sour cream	1 cup

Procedure:

1. In a heavy saucepan saute onions in olive oil until golden.

2. Add beef and cook until brown. Season with chef's salt and add tomato paste. Reduce heat, cover, and simmer about 30 minutes.

3. Add veal and pork and simmer 30 minutes more. Add white wine and cook until meat is very tender. Stir in sour cream. Serve over egg noodles.

Recommended Wine: Cabernet Franc/Pinot Noir

Budapest Goulash

Yield: 4 Portions

Ingredients	Amounts
sliced onions	4 cups
olive oil	¼ cup
Hungarian paprika	¼ cup
red wine vinegar	¼ cup
beef stew meat	2 lbs.
chef's salt	1 tbsp.
thyme	1 tsp.
tomato paste	¼ cup
garlic, minced	1 tbsp.
flour	¼ cup
beef broth	2 cups
lemon zest	1 tbsp.
caraway seeds	1 tbsp.

Procedure:

1. In a heavy saucepan saute onions in olive oil until golden.

2. Add paprika and vinegar. Cook 5 minutes and add stew meat, chef's salt and thyme. Cook until meat is brown.

3. Add tomato paste and garlic and cook until meat is glazed. Add flour and stir. Add beef broth and cook, covered, until meat is very tender (about 1 hour). Garnish with lemon zest and caraway seeds. Serve with boiled potatoes.

Recommended Wine: Cabernet Franc/Pinot Noir

Transylvanian Goulash

Yield: 4 Portions

Ingredients	Amounts
olive oil	2 tbsp.
onions, chopped	2 cups
garlic, minced	1 tsp.
paprika	¼ cup
pork cubes	2 lbs.
chicken broth	1 cup
fresh sauerkraut	1 lb.
caraway seeds	1 tbsp.
chicken broth	1 cup
tomato paste	¼ cup
sour cream	1 cup

Procedure:

1. In a heavy saucepan, saute onions in olive oil until golden. Stir in garlic and paprika.

2. Add pork and brown. Add chicken broth and bring to boil. Spread fresh sauerkraut over meat with caraway seeds.

3. Mix chicken broth with tomato paste and pour over meat. Cover and simmer until pork is tender. Skim off fat and stir in sour cream. Serve over egg noodles.

Recommended Wine: Dry Riesling

Turducken
Yield: 14 portions
Adapted from the recipe of Paul Prudhomme

Ingredients	Amounts
pancetta, ¼" dice	1 lb.
Italian sweet sausage	1½ lb.
olive oil	¼ cup
chopped onions	2 cups
chopped carrots	2 cups
chopped celery	2 cups
garlic, minced	2 tbsp..
anise seed	1 tbsp.
chicken giblets	from 1 chicken
duck giblets	from 1 duck
turkey giblets	from 1 turkey
chef's salt	to taste
brandy	½ cup
thyme	1 tbsp.
tarragon	1 tbsp.
French bread, ½" cubes	4 cups
boned 16 lb. turkey	
boned 6 lb. duck	
boned 3 lb. chicken	
lemon pepper seasoning	2 tbsp.

Procedure:

1. Bone chicken, duck, and turkey, leaving skin intact.*

2. Cook pancetta in saute pan until brown. Remove.

3. Remove sausage from casing, break into pieces, brown, remove.

4. Pour off fat. Add oil and onion, carrot, celery, anise seed. Cook 2 minutes and add giblets. Cook until giblets are almost cooked through and add brandy. Stir in thyme and tarragon. Remove giblets and chop. *(continued on next page...)*

Notes: Use a very sharp knife. Make a cut along underside of backbone. Work knife around bird, keeping close to rib cage. Cut through leg and wing joints. Use a butcher's needle to sew. If desired, ask a butcher to bone the poultry.

5. Fold together pancetta, sausage, vegetables, giblets and bread cubes. Taste for seasoning and cool in refrigerator.

6. Place layers of stuffing between boned out poultry. Sew turkey with butcher twine.

7. Season with lemon pepper seasoning.

8. Cover Turducken with foil and cook at 250°F until internal temperature reaches 130°F (about 4 hours).

9. Remove foil and baste Turducken. Turn up heat to 350°F and cook uncovered until internal temperature reaches 170°F. Baste frequently.

10. Remove from oven and let rest half an hour before carving.

Recommended Wine: Merlot or Pinot Noir

Soups
and Vegetables

Roasted Corn Chowder with Herb Butter
Yield: 8 portions, about 2 quarts

Ingredients	Amounts
corn on the cob	8 ears
olive oil	¼ cup
onion, diced	2 cups
leeks, white part, diced	1 cup
red pepper, diced	1 cup
green pepper, diced	1 cup
jalapeño pepper, minced	1 pepper
thyme	1 tsp.
bay leaf	1
salt	1 tbsp.
potatoes, diced	1 quart
chicken stock	2 quarts
heavy cream	1 cup
chopped parsley	½ cup
herb butter	1 slice per portion

Procedure:

1. Shuck corn, oil lightly, and roast in covered barbecue grill over charcoal (about 10 min.). Cool. Slice off kernels and reserve.

2. Heat olive oil in soup pot and add onion and leeks. Saute five minutes and add peppers, thyme, bay leaf and salt. Cook 5 min.

3. Add potatoes and chicken stock. Simmer until potatoes are tender. Add corn kernels, cream, and chopped parsley. Check seasoning.

4. For herb butter, soften ¼ lb. butter in a bowl and add chopped garlic, basil, parsley, chives, and lemon juice. Mash together and place on piece of tin foil. Roll foil into cylinder and refrigerate until hard. Slice off pieces and float in the soup portions.

Note: Roasting the corn over charcoal is not essential, but it creates a unique char-grilled flavor in the soup.

Pumpkin Chardonnay Soup

Yield: About 2 quarts or 8 portions

Ingredients	Amounts
olive oil	¼ cup
onion, chopped	2 cups
leeks, white part only, diced	1 cup
garlic, minced	1 tbsp.
thyme	1 tbsp.
Chardonnay	1 cup
chicken stock	6 cups
Pumpkin, peeled, seeded, and cut into one-inch cubes	6 cups
carrots, peeled, cut into chunks	1 cup
white turnip, peeled, cut into chunks	1 cup
parsnip, peeled, cut into chunks	1 cup
potato, peeled, cut up	1 cup
heavy cream	1 cup
salt	1 tbsp.
pepper	2 tsp.
nutmeg	1 tsp.
croutons for garnish	2 cups

Procedure:

1. Heat oil in soup pot. Add onion, leek, garlic, thyme. Cover and cook slowly for 5 minutes.

2. Add Chardonnay and reduce by one half.

3. Add pumpkin, carrots, turnip, parsnip, and potato. Add chicken stock. Simmer until vegetables are fully cooked (about 30 min.).

4. Strain liquid from soup and reserve. Puree cooked vegetables in food processor and add back to liquid.

5. Add cream and seasonings. Taste for salt and pepper.

6. Garnish with fresh croutons and serve.

Note: For a festive occasion, serve this soup in a hollowed out pumpkin. Toasted pumpkin seeds make an excellent garnish along with homemade croutons.

Mulligatawny Soup

Yield: 2 quarts or 8 portions

Ingredients	Amounts
onion, diced	2 cups
celery, diced	2 cups
butter	¼ lb.
eggplant, peeled, cut in ½" dice	2 cups
green pepper, diced	1 cup
red pepper, diced	1 cup
apples, peeled, cored, cut in ½" dice	2 cups
flour	½ cup
curry powder	2 tbsp.
salt/pepper	1 tbsp. each
chicken stock	6 cups
rice, cooked	2 cups
chicken meat, cooked, diced	2 cups
milk or light cream	3 cups
chopped parsley	½ cup

Procedure:

1. Saute onion and celery in butter in soup pot.

2. In separate sauce pan, boil water and add eggplant, peppers, and apple for two minutes to blanch. Drain and reserve.

3. Add flour, curry powder, salt and pepper to sauteed onion and cook for 3 minutes. Stir in chicken stock and simmer.

4. Add eggplant, peppers, and apples. Stir. Add chicken meat, rice, and milk. Check seasoning and add chopped parsley.

Polish Beet Soup with Uszka

Yield: 2 quarts

Ingredients	Amounts
dried mushrooms	3 oz.
water, boiling	1 quart
beets, peeled, grated	2½ lbs.
water	5 cups
red wine vinegar	2 tbsp.
salt	2 tsp.
salt	½ tsp.
sugar	¼ tsp.
lemon juice	1 tbsp.

Procedure:

1. Pour boiling water over mushrooms and let them soak at room temperature for 2 hours.

2. Put mushrooms and water into saucepan and simmer, uncovered, about 2 hours or until liquid is reduced to ½ cup. Drain stock and reserve mushrooms for Uszka. Reserve stock.

3. Put grated beets in a saucepan and add water. Bring to a boil and cook uncovered for 10 minutes. Add the vinegar and salt and simmer for 30 minutes. Strain beet stock, pushing hard on beets to extract juice. Discard beets.

4. Combine beet stock and mushroom stock with salt, sugar, and lemon juice. Bring to boil, check for seasoning, and serve with Uszka (see next page).

Note: Many people from the Polish community on the North Fork have worked in restaurants over the years. This recipe was taught to me by one of my employees, Anna.

Uszka Stuffing

Ingredients	Amounts
butter	6 tbsp.
onions, chopped	½ cup
soft fresh bread crumbs	1 tbsp.
cooked dried mushrooms	3 oz.
egg white	1
salt	1 tsp.

Procedure:

1. Melt 2 tbsp. butter in a saute pan, add onions and cook until soft. Stir in bread crumbs and remove from heat. Stir in mushrooms. Pulse this mixture in a food processor. Do not puree.
2. Melt 4 tbsp. butter and add mushroom mixture. Cook until most liquid has evaporated. Stir in egg white and salt. Cool.

Dough for Uszka

Ingredients	Amounts
egg, whole	1
egg white	1
cold water	1 tbsp.
salt	2¼ tsp.
flour, all purpose	1 cup

Procedure:

1. In a large bowl, beat whole egg, egg white, water and ¼ tsp. of salt until smooth. Continue beating with spoon while sifting in flour a little at a time. Knead with your hands until dough can be gathered into a ball.
2. On a floured board roll dough into thin rectangle about 15 by 9 inches. Turn dough at right angles and dust both sides with flour. Cut into 60 1½-inch squares. Cover with a damp kitchen towel.
3. To make Uszka, put ¼ tsp. of mushroom filling in center of square of dough. Dip your finger in cold water and moisten edges. Fold square in half diagonally to make a triangle. Press edges together and lift up the two points of the base and pinch together.
4. Boil 2 quarts of water with 2 tsp. salt. Drop in batches of dumplings and simmer for 5 minutes. Serve in soup bowls with beet soup.

Potato Dumplings
Yield: 8 portions

Ingredients	Amounts
potatoes, boiled, peeled	2 lbs.
flour	1 cup
salt	2 tsp.
eggs, beaten	2
butter	¼ cup
bread crumbs	½ cup

Procedure:

1. Grate potatoes into a bowl. Add flour, salt, and eggs. Mix to form a stiff dough. Add more flour if necessary.
2. Divide dough into portions about the size of a golf ball. Roll each into a ball and refrigerate about one hour.
3. Saute bread crumbs in butter until brown. Set aside.
4. Cook dumplings in boiling salted water for 10 minutes. Stir gently to prevent sticking. Remove with slotted spoon and roll in bread crumbs. Prepare mushrooms and cream:

Mushrooms and Cream

Ingredients	Amounts
white mushrooms, sliced	2 cups
crimini mushrooms (babybella) sliced	1 cup
shiitake mushrooms	1 cup
oyster mushrooms, sliced	1 cup
shallots, finely diced	1 cup
chanterelle mushrooms	1 cup
unsalted butter	½ cup
lemon juice	from one lemon
heavy cream	1 cup
salt and white pepper	to taste

Procedure:

1. Saute shallots in butter until soft. Add mushrooms and cook at medium heat until mushrooms are tender.
2. Stir in lemon juice, heavy cream, salt and pepper.
3. Pour mixture over potato dumplings and serve.

Potato Pancakes

Yield: 2 dozen small pancakes

Ingredients	Amounts
potatoes, raw, peeled	2 lbs.
onion, peeled	1 medium onion
lemon juice	1 tbsp.
eggs, beaten	2
chopped parsley	2 tbsp.
salt	1 tsp.
white pepper	½ tsp.
flour	¼ cup
oil for pan frying	as needed

Procedure:

1. Grate potatoes and onion into a bowl with a hand grater. Add lemon juice and put mixture into a strainer. Squeeze out as much liquid as possible. Hold the liquid and let the starch settle. Add starch back to potato mixture.
2. Add eggs, parsley, salt and pepper to potato mixture. Stir in flour. If mixture seems too thin, add a little more flour.
3. Heat a heavy skillet and coat with oil. Spoon in potato mixture and cook until golden brown on each side.

Leek Pancakes

Yield: 2 dozen small pancakes

Ingredients	Amounts
leeks, white part only, diced	1 cup
butter	2 tbsp.
salt	1 tsp.
egg	1
flour	½ cup
milk	½ cup

Procedure:

1. Saute the leeks in butter at low heat. Add salt, remove from pan and cool.
2. Mix together egg, flour, and milk. Stir in cooled leeks.
3. Cook pancakes in lightly oiled or nonstick saute pan. Saute each side until lightly browned.

Baked Stuffed Eggplant

Yield: 4 Portions

Ingredients	Amounts
large eggplants	2
garlic, minced	1 tbsp.
onion, diced	½ cup
zucchini, ¼" dice	1 cup
mushrooms, ¼" dice	1 cup
red pepper, ¼" dice	½ cup
green pepper, ¼" dice	½ cup
tomatoes, peeled, seeded, diced	2
cooked brown rice or	
cooked barley	2 cups
goat cheese	4 oz. (1 log)
pimiento	to garnish
olives	to garnish
olive oil	2 tbsp.
salt/pepper	to taste
oregano	1 tbsp.

Procedure:

1. Slice eggplants in half lengthwise. Cut around edge with paring knife, leaving ¼" wall. Scoop out insides and chop.

2. Saute eggplant, garlic, onion, zucchini, mushrooms, peppers and tomato in olive oil for 5 minutes. Season with salt, pepper and oregano. Combine with cooked rice or barley and stuff into eggplant shells.

3. Top with goat cheese slices and garnish with strips of pimiento and olives.

4. Place on sheet pan in 350°F oven for 20 minutes.

Note: Serve on a bed of wilted greens such as spinach, broccoli rabe, arugula or swiss chard.

Braised Red Cabbage

Yield: 8 portions

Ingredients	Amounts
red cabbage, cored, sliced thin	2 heads (about 2 lbs.)
bacon, diced	3 strips
onions, sliced	2 cups
sugar	1 tbsp.
chicken broth	½ cup
apples, cored, diced, skin left on	2 cups
whole cloves	4
stick cinnamon	1
allspice, ground	½ tsp
red wine vinegar	¼ cup
red wine	½ cup
salt and pepper	to taste

Procedure:

1. In a sautoir or brazier, brown bacon and add onions and sugar. Cook until onions are soft.

2. Add sliced cabbage and stir to coat. Add chicken broth, apples, cloves, cinnamon, and allspice. (Tie spices in cheesecloth if desired.) Cover and simmer for 30 minutes.

3. Add vinegar and red wine. Simmer another 15 minutes. Season to taste with salt and pepper.

North Fork Vegetable Ragout

Yield: 8 portions

Ingredients	Amounts
mushrooms, quartered	2 cups
zucchini, ½" dice	2 cups
green peppers, ½" dice	1 cup
red peppers, ½" dice	1 cups
eggplant, peeled, ½" dice	2 cups
yellow squash, ½" dice	1 cup
garlic, minced	2 tbsp.
tomatoes, peeled, seeded, chopped	2 cups
olive oil	¼ cup
parsley, chopped	¼ cup
basil, chopped, fresh	¼ cup
bay leaf	1
salt	1 tbsp.
pepper	2 tsp.
croutons	1 cup
spaghetti squash	2
Jack 'B' Little pumpkins	8

Procedure:

1. Cut spaghetti squash in half lengthwise and place cut side down on lightly oiled sheet pan. Put whole Jack 'B' Little pumpkins on same pan and roast in 300°F oven until tender (45 minutes). Remove and cool.

2. In large sautoir or brazier heat olive oil and add all ingredients except croutons. Cook at medium heat, stirring, until vegetables are just tender. Stir in croutons and check for seasoning.

3. Cut tops off pumpkins and scrape out seeds with a spoon. Stuff each pumpkin with vegetable mixture. Remove seeds from the center of spaghetti squash and scrape out flesh with a dinner fork.

4. On a sheet pan make eight small piles of spaghetti squash. Place a stuffed pumpkin on each one. Surround them with remaining vegetables and heat in oven. Serve on plates.

Long Grain Wild Rice Pilaf

Yield: 4 portions

Ingredients	Amounts
long grain wild rice	1 cup
chicken broth	4 cups
butter	½ cup
onion, chopped	½ cup
celery, sliced on bias	½ cup
mushrooms, sliced	1 cup
ground black pepper	1 tsp.

Procedure:

1. Combine wild rice and chicken broth in a saucepan. Bring to a boil, cover, reduce heat to a simmer and cook 45 minutes.

2. In saute pan, melt butter and saute onions, celery, and mushrooms. Season with black pepper and add to cooked wild rice.

Notes: Saute 1 tbsp. of garlic with onions if desired. Use chopped portabello mushroom stems instead of white mushrooms. Roast the portabello caps for 15 minutes in a 350°F oven and stuff them with the wild rice mixture. This makes a great accompaniment to grilled filet mignon or by itself as a vegetarian entree.

Desserts, Pastry
and Bread

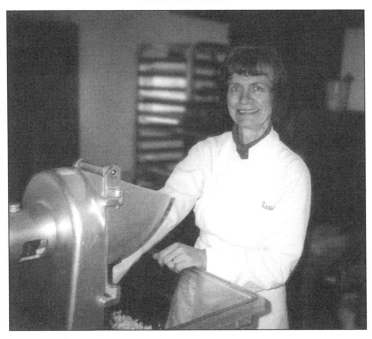

Pastry Chef Bonnie Hoffner prepared the baked products at Ross' North Fork for over 25 years. Our bakeshop philosophy, like our overall food strategy, was to keep it as simple as possible, emphasize seasonal and local products, and start from scratch.

Consequently, Bonnie made our version of Cornell formula bread — which was a yeast dough containing wheat germ, milk and honey — almost daily. She also made incredible pie pastry and puff pastry. Our pecan pie, peach blueberry pie, French apple pie, and pumpkin chiffon pie were signature desserts. In the early years, our cheesecake with apricot glaze was popular, and in the later years our lemon bars, cobblers and crisps. Perhaps our earliest dessert was our French style rice pudding.

Bonnie also made fresh pasta, biscuits, shortbreads, and many special occasion cakes. The following recipes are a sampling of our recipe file. Enjoy!

Rice Pudding

Yield: 10 portions

Ingredients	Amounts
rice	1¼ cups
milk	2½ quarts
salt	1 tsp.
eggs	5
sugar	1½ cups
cream or half and half	¾ cup
vanilla extract	1 tsp.
sugar ⎤	½ cup
cinammon ⎬ mixed	2 tbsp.
nutmeg ⎦	1 tsp.

Procedure:

1. Simmer rice, milk, and salt in heavy saucepan until very thick (about 1 hour). Stir often, cook until very thick bubbles appear.

2. Mix eggs, sugar, cream, and vanilla in bowl. Add to thick rice mixture and cook for two minutes.

3. Place in serving pan (or custard cups) and sprinkle with mixture of sugar, cinnamon, and nutmeg.

Notes: For a caramelized crust, place pan under hot broiler for 3 minutes.

Most any kind of white rice can be used. I prefer Jasmine rice due to its flowery bouquet. A medium grain rice will give a creamy texture. This is one of the simplest and best dessert recipes that I've ever seen. The secret is to cook it slowly until very thick. If desired, add raisins at the end.

Pie Crust Pastry

Yield: Two 9" pie crusts

Ingredients	Amounts
flour, all purpose	2 cups
salt	½ tsp.
shortening	⅔ cup
cold water	½ cup

Procedure:

1. Measure flour and salt into bowl.
2. Cut in shortening with pastry blender (or two knives, or fingers).
3. Sprinkle half the water over dry ingredients and stir lightly with a fork.
4. Add remaining water and stir with fork. Form into 2 balls of equal size. Roll out on floured board to make 2 pie crusts (fits 9" tin).

Quick Puff Pastry

Ingredients	Amounts
flour, all purpose	2 cups
cold butter, cut in small pieces	1 lb.
ice water	1 cup

Procedure:

1. Combine flour and cold butter in a mixing bowl. Cut butter into flour with a pastry blender or your hands.
2. Mix in water gradually to make a rough dough.
3. Place dough on a floured surface. Roll into a rectangle ½" thick. Fold a quarter of dough from top to center. Fold a quarter of dough from bottom to center. Fold in half to make 4 layers.
4. Make sure dough is cold. Roll into rectangle 6"x18". Fold dough into thirds. Turn dough a quarter turn and repeat, rolling into a rectangle three times.
5. Chill dough for 30 minutes. Cut dough in half and roll out ⅛" thick. Cut into desired shapes.
6. Preheat oven to 425°. Place puff pastry on parchment-lined sheet pans and bake about 20 minutes.

Pecan Pie

Yield: Two 9" pies

Ingredients	Amounts
pecan pieces	2 cups
eggs	6
sugar	1⅓ cups
salt	1 tsp.
butter, melted	⅔ cup
dark corn syrup	2 cups

Procedure:

1. Prepare two unbaked pie shells with high fluted edge (see recipe on previous page.)

2. Sprinkle one cup of pecans in each shell.

3. Beat eggs in bowl. Stir in sugar, salt, melted butter, and dark corn syrup.

4. Pour mixture over pecans and bake at 375° for 30 minutes or until custard is set.

Hot Fudge Pecan Pie

Yield: Two 9" Pies

Ingredients	Amounts
flour, all purpose	1¾ cups
confectioners sugar	½ cup
cocoa	½ cup
salt	½ tsp.
cold butter, cut in pieces	6 oz.
cold water	¼ cup (approx.)

Procedure:

1. Combine flour, sugar, cocoa, and salt in food processor. Process briefly and add butter pieces.
2. Pulse until mixture resembles coarse meal. Transfer to a bowl and toss with cold water until dough clings together.
3. Divide in half, form two balls and flatten them into rounds. Cover with plastic wrap and refrigerate 30 minutes. Roll out and place in two 9" pie tins.

Filling

Ingredients	Amounts
eggs, lightly beaten	6
dark corn syrup	2 cups
sugar	⅔ cup
butter	2 oz.
semi-sweet chocolate	8 oz.
vanilla	2 tsp.
pecan pieces	3 cups

Procedure:

1. Melt butter and chocolate in a saucepan. Add eggs, corn syrup, sugar and vanilla. Stir with wooden spoon.
2. Sprinkle pecan pieces into two pie shells. Pour chocolate mixture over them and bake at 350°F for 50-60 minutes (insert knife in center, it should come out clean.) Cool and refrigerate.

Note: Serve this pie warm with chocolate ice cream and hot fudge sauce.

French Apple Pie

Yield: One 9" pie

Ingredients	Amounts
pie pastry, uncooked (recipe p. 95)	one 9" crust
sugar	1 cup
corn starch	2 tbsp.
cinnamon	1 tsp
apples (peeled, cored, sliced)	6 cups
lemon juice	1 tbsp.
vanilla	1 tsp.
butter	2 tbsp.

Crumb Topping

Ingredients	Amounts
flour, all purpose	1 cup
salt	½ tsp
sugar	¼ cup
brown sugar	¼ cup
butter, cut in small pieces	½ cup

Procedure:

1. Combine sugar, cinnamon, cornstarch, and apples in a bowl and let stand.

2. Combine topping ingredients (except the butter) in food processor. Turn on processor and add cold butter pieces. Mixture will resemble coarse cornmeal.

3. Mix lemon juice and vanilla into apple mixture. Place in pie shell and dot with butter.

4. Sprinkle topping over apples and bake at 450°F for 10 minutes. Lower heat to 375°F and bake 40 minutes.

Apple-Cranberry-Raisin Pie

Yield: 8 portions

Ingredients	Amounts
tart cooking apples	
peeled, cored, cut in chunks	5 cups
fresh cranberries	1 cup
golden raisins	½ cup
sugar	½ cup
salt	¼ tsp.
flour	2 tbsp.
butter	2 tbsp.
grated lemon zest	1 tbsp.
uncooked double crust	
9" pie shell	(recipe, p. 95)

Procedure:

1. Place apples, cranberries, and raisins in a bowl. Add sugar, salt, and flour. Toss together and turn into pie crust.

2. Dot fruit with butter and lemon zest. Put on top crust, flute, and sprinkle with sugar.

3. Bake at 400°F for about 30 minutes or golden brown.

Notes: Mutsu, Ida Red, Braeburn, or Jonagold apples from the North Fork are best.

Pear or Apple Tarte Tatin

Yield: One 10" tarte

Ingredients	Amounts
flour, all purpose	1½ cups
butter, cold, cut in small pieces	3½ ounces
salt	½ tsp.
sugar	2 tsp.
egg yolk	1
cold water	4 tbsp.
pears or apples, peeled, cored	
cut in quarters	6-8
butter	6 ounces
sugar	2 cups

Procedure:

1. Combine flour, sugar, and salt in bowl of mixer. Add cut up butter and mix with paddle just until butter is coated with flour.
   Combine egg yolk and water and add to mixer. Mix until it resembles coarse crumbs.

2. Turn out on floured board and knead for two minutes. Shape
   into a round disc and chill.

3. Melt butter and sugar in 10" cast iron skillet until sugar begins to
   carmelize. Place fruit in pan in a tightly packed single layer.
   Cook on top of stove until a deep caramel color is formed and
   sauce is thick.

4. Roll out pastry to size slightly larger than pan. Set pastry on top
   of fruit and bake at 425°F until pastry is golden brown (20 min.).

5. Let cool for 10 minutes and turn out onto a plate. Cut into 8 wedges.

Note: It is important to let fruit cook long enough to evapo-
rate liquid and caramelize sugar (20 min. or more). After it
cools, cover pan tightly with a plate. Flip it over quickly
while holding plate on tight. Scrape any excess fruit out of
pan.

Peach Blueberry Pie

Yield: 8 portions

Ingredients	Amounts
peaches, peeled and sliced	5 cups
blueberries	1 cup
tapioca	3 tbsp.
sugar	1 cup
salt	½ tsp.
lemon juice	1 tbsp.
butter	2 tbsp.
uncooked 9" double pie crust	(recipe, p. 95)

Procedure:

1. Place peaches and blueberries in bowl with lemon juice.

2. Combine tapioca, sugar, and salt and add to fruit.

3. Turn fruit mixture into pie shell and dot with butter.

4. Cover with lattice or plain pie crust and flute edges.

5. Bake at 400° for about 45 minutes or until golden brown.

Peach Blueberry Cobbler

Yield: 15 portions

Ingredients	Amounts
peaches, peeled and sliced	5 quarts
blueberries	3 cups
cornstarch	½ cup
sugar	3 cups
salt	2 tsp.
lemon juice	¼ cup
vanilla extract	1 tbsp.

Procedure:

1. Combine all ingredients in a large bowl and toss together.
2. Transfer to a 12" x 20" x 2" deep pan (hotel pan) and set aside.

Biscuit Topping

Ingredients	Amounts
flour, all purpose	3 cups
sugar	⅓ cup
baking powder	1½ tsp.
salt	¾ tsp.
butter, cut in pieces	6 oz.
milk	1½ cups

Procedure:

1. Combine flour, sugar, baking powder, and salt in a bowl. Stir with whisk.
2. Add cold butter pieces and cut them in with your hands or a pastry blender. It should resemble corn meal.
3. Stir in milk with wooden spoon to make dough. Do not overmix.
4. Using a scoop or two spoons, spoon 15 portions of dough on top of fruit in hotel pan.
5. Bake at 400°F for about 40 minutes. Biscuits should be lightly brown and cooked in the center.

Note: You can subsitute fresh raspberries for the blueberries if desired.

Pumpkin Chiffon Pie

Yield: 8 portions

Ingredients	Amounts
baked pie crusts (recipe. p. 95)	2
unflavored gelatin	2 tbsp.
brown sugar	1⅓ cups
ground nutmeg	1 tsp.
ground cinnamon	1 tsp.
salt	1 tsp.
ground ginger	¼ tsp.
egg yolks	6
egg whites	6
milk	1 cup
fresh pureed pumpkin	2 cups
sugar	¾ cup
heavy cream	2 cups

Procedure:

1. Make pie crusts with high fluted edge and bake until golden brown. Cool.

2. Cut and peel fresh pumpkin into cubes, simmer in water until tender, and puree in food processor. Strain out excess water. Cool.

3. In a saucepan combine gelatin, brown sugar, nutmeg, cinnamon, salt, and ginger. Stir with whisk.

4. Whisk together egg yolks, milk and pumpkin puree. Add to saucepan with above mixture and cook over medium heat until it comes to a boil. Pour into bowl and cool to room temperature.

5. Beat egg whites until soft peaks form. Beat in sugar and fold into pumpkin mixture.

6. Beat heavy cream until stiff. Fold into pumpkin mixture.

7. Pour into pie crusts and chill until firm.

Note: You will need about 4 cups of fresh pumpkin to get 2 cups of puree.

Irish Coffee Fudge Pie

Yield: Two 9" pies

Ingredients	Amounts
chocolate wafer crumbs	2½ cups
sugar	2 tbsp.
melted butter	½ cup
evaporated milk	2 cups
minature marshmallows	2 cups
semi-sweet chocolate chips	2 cups
coffee ice cream	8 cups
Kahlua (or coffee liqueur)	2 tbsp.

Procedure:

1. Combine wafer crumbs, sugar, and melted butter in a bowl. Divide between two 9" pie tins. Press crumbs against bottom and sides of tins, using the back of a spoon. Bake in 375°F oven for 10 minutes. Cool and put in freezer.

2. Combine evaporated milk, marshmallows, and chocolate chips in a saucepan and cook at low heat until melted. Chill.

3. Soften ice cream and stir in coffee liqueur. Spread ice cream on bottom of each pie shell. Spread layer of fudge sauce on top. Repeat ice cream layer and fudge sauce layer. Freeze until service.

Ross' Ice Cream Pie

Yield: Two 9" Pies

Ingredients	Amounts
melted butter	½ cup
chocolate wafer crumbs	2½ cups
raspberry sherbet	4 cups
chocolate ice cream	4 cups
lime sherbet	4 cups

Procedure:

1. Combine wafer crumbs and melted butter in a bowl. Press into two pie tins with the back of a spoon. Bake at 375° for about 10 minutes. Cool and place in freezer.

2. Soften raspberry sherbet and spread into pie shells. Freeze for 12 minutes. Repeat with chocolate ice cream and finish with lime sherbet.

Pie Variations

Other flavors of ice cream can be substituted. A "creamsickle pie" with orange sherbet and vanilla ice cream is very good. Garnish it by melting ½ cup of chocolate chips with 1 tbsp. of salad oil and drizzling onto the top of the pies with a swirling motion.

Norwegian Feast Cake

Yield: 12 portions

Ingredients	Amounts
eggs, large	4
sugar, granulated	1⅓ cups
water	½ cup
flour (all purpose)	1½ cups
baking powder	1 heaping tsp.

Procedure:

1. Preheat oven to 350°F and lightly grease and flour the bottom of a 10" springform pan.

2. Using electric mixer with whisk, beat eggs and sugar together for 15 min. (use a timer or clock).

3. Meanwhile sift flour and baking powder together. Set aside.

4. Gradually add water to egg mixture, beating with mixer at low speed.

5. Gradually add flour mixture (about ½ cup at a time) beating at low speed. *Do not overbeat.* Pour into prepared pan and bake at 350°F for 30 mins. It's done when center springs back to touch. Cool on rack 10 min. and remove sides of pan. Cool thoroughly.

Notes: This cake is usually cut into 3 layers. Spread whipped cream between layers along with fresh seasonal fruit: strawberries, blueberries, peaches or a combination.

This cake also makes a very good version of Baked Alaska. Split cake in half, spread ice cream about one inch thick. Cover with top of cake. Cover entire cake with meringue and freeze. At service time, place in a hot oven (425°F) until meringue browns (5 min.). Warm brandy on stove, pour over cake, and ignite with a match.

Chocolate Sheet Cake with Chocolate Frosting

Yield: 12x18x1 Sheet Cake

Ingredients	Amounts
flour, all purpose	3 cups
sugar	2 cups
cocoa	½ cup
baking soda	2 tsp.
salt	1 tsp.
water	2 cups
salad oil	¾ cup
vinegar, white	2 tbsp.
vanilla extract	2 tsp.

Procedure:

1. Line 12"x18"x1" sheet pan with foil. Preheat oven to 350°F.

2. Combine flour, sugar, cocoa, baking soda and salt. Stir with wire whisk.

3. Combine water, oil, vinegar, and vanilla in another bowl. Add to dry ingredients and mix with a wire whisk for 3 minutes.

4. Pour into pan, level with a spatula and bake for 30 minutes. Remove and cool for 15 minutes. Turn upside down onto a clean sheet pan. Remove foil and cut in half to make two layers.

Chocolate Frosting

Ingredients	Amounts
semi sweet chocolate	6 oz.
heavy cream	½ cup
butter	1 cup
confectioners sugar, sifted	2½ cups

Procedure:

1. In a saucepan, combine chocolate, cream and butter. Cook over medium heat until melted and smooth.

2. Remove from heat and whisk in confectioners sugar.

3. Cool in refrigerator, stirring occasionally until frosting holds its shape.

Ross' Cheesecake and Apricot Glaze
Yield: 12 portions

Ingredients	Amounts
butter, melted	2 tbsp.
graham cracker crumbs	¼ cup
cream cheese (at room temp.)	2 lbs.
eggs, large	4
sugar, granulated	1¾ cups
vanilla	1 tsp.
juice and grated rind of 1 lemon	

Procedure:

1. Coat bottom of 3 qt. souffle dish with butter and sprinkle with crumbs.

2. Place the remaining ingredients in bowl of electric mixer. Use whisk. Beat at low speed for 2 minutes. Scrape bowl. Increase speed to high and beat until evenly blended, scraping bowl as needed.

3. Pour batter into prepared pan.

4. Set pan inside a roasting pan and place in 350°F preheated oven. Pour boiling water into roasting pan to depth of ½".

5. Bake at 350°F for about 1¼ hrs. or until cake is set in the middle. Turn off oven and let cake rest with door closed for 20 min.

6. Remove cake to cooling rack and cool to room temperature.

Apricot Glaze

Combine 10 oz. apricot jam, ¼ cup water, ¼ cup sugar and 1 tbsp. apricot brandy in a small saucepan and bring to the boil, stirring. Pour over cheesecake slices. Garnish with apricot halves.

Lemon Bars

Yield: 8 portions

Ingredients	Amounts
flour, all purpose	2 cups
sugar	½ cup
lemon zest, grated	1 tsp.
butter, cut in 1" pieces	1 cup
eggs	4
lemon juice	½ cup
flour	⅓ cup
baking powder	½ tsp.
sugar	1½ cups
lemon zest, grated	1 tsp.

Procedure:

1. Combine flour, sugar, lemon zest in food processor. Add butter pieces and pulse to form coarse crumb mixture. Pat mixture into 13" x 9" x 2" baking pan. Bake in 350° oven about 20 minutes or until light brown.

2. Combine in food processor eggs, lemon juice, flour, baking powder, sugar, and lemon zest. Process about 10 seconds, scraping down bowl with spatula. Pour over partially baked crust and return to 350°F oven and bake 20 minutes. Cool on wire rack. Cut in squares or triangles and serve.

Note: Serve this with lemon sorbet or vanilla ice cream. Garnish with lemon slice.

Rhubarb Crunch

Yield: 8 portions

Ingredients	Amounts
rhubarb, fresh, ½" dice	8 cups
flour	1½ cups
uncooked old fashioned oatmeal	1¼ cups
brown sugar	1 cup
melted butter	6 oz.
cinnamon	1 tbsp.
sugar	1½ cups
cornstarch	3 tbsp.
water	1½ cups
vanilla extract	1 tsp.

Procedure:

1. Mix flour, oatmeal, brown sugar and cinnamon in a bowl. Stir in melted butter to form crumbly mixture.

2. In a saucepan combine sugar, cornstarch, water, and vanilla. Bring to a boil and cook until thickened, stirring slowly. Add diced rhubarb to this sauce.

3. Sprinkle half of the oatmeal mixture into a 9" x 13" baking pan with 2" sides. Pour rhubarb mixture over it and top with remaining oatmeal mixture.

4. Bake at 350°F for about 45 minutes or until rhubarb is bubbling and tender. Serve with vanilla ice cream.

Apple Cranberry Crisp
Yield: 10 portions

Ingredients	Amounts
apples, peeled, cored, sliced	1 gallon
cranberries	3 cups
brown sugar	1 cup
cornstarch	⅓ cup
cinnamon	4 tsp.
nutmeg	1 tsp
grated orange rind	1 tbsp.
orange juice	½ cup
flour	3 cups
oatmeal, old fashioned	1½ cups
brown sugar	1 lb.
ground ginger	1 tsp.
butter, cut in small pieces	½ lb.

Procedure:

1. Combine apples, cranberries, brown sugar, cornstarch, cinnamon, nutmeg, orange rind and juice in stainless bowl. Stir and place in shallow baking pan.

2. To make topping, combine dry ingredients in a food processor. Pulse to mix and add butter pieces. Pulse to form crumbly mixture. Sprinkle over fruit and bake at 325°F about 30 minutes.

Notes: The North Fork produces many fine apple varieties. Perhaps the best for cooking are Mutsu and Ida Red. But varieties such as Jonagold and Empire are delicious to mix in. Traditional Granny Smith's and Greenings are also very good.

Orange Truffle Mousse
Yield: 8 portions

Ingredients	Amounts
unflavored gelatin	1 envelope
orange juice	½ cup
egg yolks	5
egg whites	5
superfine sugar	½ cup
grated orange zest	1 tsp.
Grand Marnier	3 tbsp.
heavy cream	1 cup
cream of tartar	½ tsp.

Chocolate Truffles

Ingredients	Amounts
semi-sweet chocolate	6 oz.
butter	4 tbsp.
vanilla extract	½ tsp.
egg yolks, beaten	2
cocoa	4 tbsp.

Procedure:

1. Sprinkle gelatin over orange juice in a small bowl to soften. Place bowl in hot water to dissolve gelatin.

2. In a double boiler at low heat, beat egg yolks and sugar about five minutes. Remove from heat and continue beating until mixture cools and thickens. Stir in orange zest, Grand Marnier, and gelatin mixture.

3. Beat the heavy cream until it forms soft peaks. In a separate bowl beat the egg whites with cream of tartar until they form soft peaks.

4. Place bowl of orange mixture in ice bath and stir until slightly thickened. Fold in cream and egg whites with spatula.

Truffles:

1. Melt the chocolate and butter in a double boiler. Remove from heat and stir in vanilla. Temper egg yolks with a little warm chocolate, then add yolks to chocolate mixture and stir. Chill for one hour, covered.

2. Form tablespoons of chocolate mixture into balls and roll them in cocoa. Refrigerate.

Assembly:

Spoon about ½ cup of mousse into stem glass serving dish. Place one truffle in center and cover with mousse. Refrigerate two hours. Serve with whipped cream and orange zest.

Fourth of July Mousse
Yield: 8 portions

Ingredients	Amounts
plain gelatin	1 tbsp.
salt	dash
sugar	¼ cup
egg yolks	2
egg whites	2
milk	1¼ cups
vanilla extract	½ tsp.
sugar	¼ cup
heavy cream	1 cup

Procedure:

1. Mix gelatin and salt with sugar in a saucepan.
2. Separate eggs. Beat egg yolks together with milk. Add this to saucepan with gelatin and cook over low heat until gelatin is dissolved (5 min.) Remove from heat and add vanilla. Chill until mixture begins to thicken.
3. Beat egg whites until foamy and gradually beat in sugar until stiff peaks form. Fold into gelatin mixture.
4. Beat heavy cream until stiff and fold into gelatin mixture.
5. Spoon into large red wine glasses or clear glass bowls. Leave room for sauce and blueberries.

Raspberry Sauce

Ingredients	Amounts
raspberries	½ pint
currant jelly	¼ cup
sugar	2 tsp.
cornstarch	1 tsp.
blueberries	½ pint

Combine one cup fresh raspberries with ¼ cup currant jelly and 2 tsp. sugar in saucepan. Bring to a boil. Process in food processor and strain to remove seeds. Mix 1 tsp. cornstarch with 1 tbsp. cold water and add to raspberry mixture in saucepan. Cook until thick. Cool. Pour sauce over mousse and garnish with fresh blueberries.

Dark Chocolate Mousse
Yield: 8 portions

Ingredients	Amounts
semi-sweet chocolate	12 oz.
heavy cream	¾ cup
water	¼ cup
heavy cream	1¾ cups
confectioners sugar	¼ cup

Procedure:

1. Heat chocolate, cream, and water in double boiler. Stir until blended, remove from heat and cool to room temp.

2. Beat heavy cream until stiff and fold in confectioners sugar. Combine with chocolate mixture and chill.

White Chocolate Mousse
Yield: 8 portions

Ingredients	Amounts
white chocolate	12 oz.
heavy cream	¾ cup
heavy cream	1½ cups

Procedure:

1. Heat chocolate and ¾ cup of cream in double boiler. Stir until blended, remove from heat and cool to room temperature.

2. Beat 1½ cups of heavy cream until stiff and fold into chocolate mixture. Cool in refrigerator.

Notes: Serve in shallow glass dish using an ice cream scoop. Serve with a scoop of black raspberry ice cream or sorbet if desired.

Butter Rum Sauce

Yield: 1 pint

Ingredients	Amounts
butter	8 oz. (1 cup)
brown sugar	1 cup
granulated sugar	1 cup
heavy cream	1 cup
rum	½ cup

Procedure:

Combine all ingredients in a saucepan and bring to a boil. Simmer 2 minutes.

Serve with apple desserts, cakes and brownies.

Bourbon Sauce

Yield: 1½ cups

Ingredients	Amounts
butter, softened	4 oz.
sugar	½ cup
eggs	2
bourbon	1 cup

Procedure:

1. Cream butter and sugar with wire whisk until fluffy. Beat in eggs.

2. Transfer to double boiler and stir in bourbon; cook until thickened.

Serve with fruit desserts, cake and brownies.

Cherry Sauce

Yield: 2 cups

Ingredients	Amounts
canned pitted sour cherries in juice	2 cans (#303)
sugar	⅓ cup
Cherry Heering liqueur	
or flavored brandy	¼ cup
salt	½ tsp.
cornstarch	2 tbsp.
lemon juice	2 tbsp.
almond extract	few drops

Procedure:

1. Drain cherries, reserving juice. Combine juice in saucepan with sugar, Cherry Heering and salt (you should have 1½ cups — if not, add a little water). Bring to a boil.

2. Dissolve cornstarch in lemon juice and stir into above mixture. Cook until thickened and add cherries and almond extract. Chill if desired.

Melba Sauce

Yield: 2 cups

Ingredients	Amounts
raspberries, fresh	2 cups
currant jelly	½ cup
sugar	1 tbsp.
cornstarch	1 tsp.
water	1 tbsp.

Procedure:

1. Combine raspberries, currant jelly and sugar in a sauce pan. Bring to a boil.

2. Process in a food processor and strain to remove seeds. Pour back into sauce pan. Mix cornstarch and water and stir into raspberries. Cook until thickened.

Fudge Sauce
Yield: 1 cup

Ingredients	Amounts
sugar	1 cup
cocoa	1½ cups
light corn syrup	1 cup
heavy cream	½ cup
salt	¼ cup
butter	3 tbsp.
vanilla extract	1 tsp.

Procedure:

1. Combine all ingredients except vanilla into a saucepan. Cook, stirring constantly, until mixture comes to a boil. Continue cooking for 3 minutes.

2. Remove from heat and add vanilla. Serve warm, or at room temperature if desired.

Lemon Sauce
Yield: 1 cup

Ingredients	Amounts
sugar	½ cup
cornstarch	2 tsp.
salt	dash
nutmeg	dash
water	1 cup
egg yolks	2
butter	2 tbsp.
grated lemon zest	½ tsp.
lemon juice	2 tbsp.

Procedure:

1. Combine sugar, cornstarch, salt and nutmeg. Whisk dry ingredients into cold water in a saucepan. Bring to a boil.

2. Temper egg yolks with a little hot mixture, then add to saucepan. Cook one minute. Remove from heat and stir in butter, lemon zest, and lemon juice.

118

Homemade Bread

When I opened Ross' North Fork Restaurant in 1973, I made the decision that the menu would be simple and that we would only serve fresh made-from-scratch foods. This included the bread. I had just graduated from the Cornell Hotel School and was familar with Cornell Bread.

Cornell Bread was developed by Clive McKay, Professor of Animal Nutrition at the AG school. His research concerned the effect of nutrition on the life span of animals and fish. His studies in the early 1940's concluded that people's health could be improved with a more nutritious bread — one that would provide abundant minerals, vitamins and proteins with a minimum of calories and no additives. In 1955, Jeanette McKay, professor McKay's widow, published a book of recipes entitled *You Can Make Cornell Bread*. We made Cornell bread at Ross' for 27 years. In addition to being nutritious, we just like it for its texture and flavor. Our pastry chef, Bonnie Hoffner, rolled out and kneaded thousands of loaves over the years.

Except for the first recipe, the following are small quantity recipes taken from Jeanette McKay's book.

Cornell Formula Bread

Yield: 30 10 oz. loaves

Ingredients	Amounts
active dry yeast	½ cup
honey	½ cup
warm water	15 cups
hi gluten bread flour	36 cups
soy flour	2½ cups
nonfat dry milk	3¾ cups
wheat germ	1 cup
salt	⅓ cup
oil	½ cup

Procedure:

1. Place water, yeast, and honey in mixing bowl.

2. Mix together bread flour, soy flour, dry milk, and wheat germ in a bowl. Add about two-thirds of these ingredients to yeast mixture. Mix with dough hook for 2 minutes on first speed.

3. Add salt and oil.

4. Add remaining dry ingredients and mix for 10 minutes (bowl will clean up and dough will be smooth and elastic.)

5. Add 2 tbsp. of oil to finished dough and loosen from mixing bowl. Proof in warm place until dough doubles in size (about 45 minutes).

6. Punch dough, turn out on floured surface and weigh into 10 oz. pieces. Knead by hand and let rest 15 min.

7. Make loaves and place in greased loaf pans (10 oz.) Let rise in pans and bake in 325° F oven about 30 minutes.

Note: This is the large quantity recipe adapted to our needs at Ross'. The quantity of flour is variable.

Cornell 'White' Bread

Yield: 3 loaves

Ingredients	Amounts
bread flour	6 cups
wheat germ	3 tbsp.
soy flour	½ cup
non-fat dry milk	¾ cup
active dry yeast	2 tbsp.
warm water (120°F)	3 cups
honey	2 tbsp.
salt	3 tsp.
vegetable oil	2 tbsp.

Procedure:

1. Sift together the flour, wheat germ, soy flour, dry milk and yeast.

2. In a large bowl combine the water, honey, salt, and oil. Stir the liquids with a wooden spoon and add about three- fourths of the flour mixture. Beat with the spoon about three minutes. Gradually add remainder of the flour mixture.

3. Knead the above mixture in the bowl for five minutes by hand. Turn it out onto a floured board and knead. Add up to one more cup of flour if necessary to make a smooth dough.

4. Place in a lightly oiled bowl, cover with a towel, and let it rise until double in size, about 45 minutes. Punch the dough down, turn over and let rise another 20 minutes.

5. Turn dough onto board and divide into three portions. Fold each into the center to make smooth tight balls. Cover with a towel and let rest 10 minutes.

6. Shape into three loaves or cut into rolls. To shape a loaf, flatten ball of dough on the board into a rectangle. Fold each long side to the center. Flatten and fold sides to

121

center. Then roll this small rectangle to make a loaf. Press ends to seal. Either place in a greased tin (8" x 4½" x 3") or place on a sheet pan. If desired, cut into small balls and flatten to make rolls. Use the same procedure used for loaves.

7. Let loaves (or rolls) rest until double in size. Bake in a 350°F oven about 50 minutes.* Bread is done when brown on the bottom. When tapped, it should sound hollow. Remove from oven and let cool on a rack. Brush with melted butter if desired.

*If making rolls, bake about 20 minutes.

Cornell 'Whole Wheat' Bread

Yield: 2 loaves

Ingredients	Amounts
whole wheat flour	4½ cups
soy flour	½ cup
non-fat dry milk	¾ cup
wheat germ	3 tbsp.
active dry yeast	2 tbsp.
salt	2 tsp.
sesame seed	2 tsp.
walnuts, chopped	3 tbsp.
raisins	¼ cup
brown sugar	¼ cup
dark molasses	¼ cup
warm water (120°F)	2 cups
egg	1

Procedure:

1. Combine flour, soy flour, dry milk, wheat germ, yeast, salt, sesame seed, walnuts, and raisins.

2. In a large bowl, stir together brown sugar, molasses, water, and egg. Add dry ingredients to liquid gradually with a wooden spoon. Beat for 5 minutes.

3. Turn onto floured board and knead. Add more flour if necessary. Shape into a smooth ball. Place in lightly oiled bowl, cover with a towel, and let rise until double in size, about 45 minutes.

4. Bake in a 350°F oven about 50 minutes. Bread is done when brown on the bottom. When tapped, it should sound hollow.

Cornell 'Oatmeal' Bread

Yield: 3 loaves

Ingredients	Amounts
old fashioned oatmeal	2 cups
salad oil	3 tbsp.
salt	3 tsp.
honey	⅓ cup
sesame seed	¼ cup
raisins	1 cup
boiling water	3 cups
bread flour	4 cups
rye flour	1 cup
wheat germ	2 tbsp.
soy flour	½ cup
nonfat dry milk	¾ cup
active dry yeast	2 tbsp.

Procedure:

1. Bring 3 cups of water to a boil and pour into a large bowl. Add oatmeal, oil, salt, honey, sesame seed, and raisins. Let this mixture cool until it reaches about 120°F.

2. Combine bread flour, rye flour, wheat germ, soy flour, dry milk and yeast. Mix with wire whisk.

3. Stir half of dry mixture into oatmeal mixture. Beat with a wooden spoon. Mix in remainder of dry ingredients. Stir until dough becomes firm. Turn out on floured board and knead. Add more flour if necessary.

4. Place dough in lightly oiled bowl, cover with a towel, and let rise until double in size, about 25 minutes.

5. Bake in a 350°F oven about 50 minutes. Bread is done when brown on the bottom. When tapped, it should sound hollow.

Garlic Knots

Yield: About 4 dozen Knots

Ingredients	Amounts
active dry yeast	2 tbsp.
warm water	2 cups
sugar	2 tbsp.
flour, all purpose	2 lbs.
salt	2 tsp.
olive oil	6 tbsp.
garlic cloves	6
olive oil	1 cup
grated Parmesan cheese	½ cup
salt	1 tsp.

Procedure:

1. Combine water, yeast, and sugar in 5 qt. mixing bowl.

2. Add half the flour and mix with dough hook on low speed, scraping bowl occasionally. Add oil and salt and mix with dough.

3. Add the remaining flour to make a stiff dough. Knead for 10 minutes till smooth and elastic. Divide dough in 4 equal pieces, form into balls and place on a sheet pan. Brush each with oil and cover with plastic film. Let rise until double in size.

4. Place a ball of dough on lightly floured surface. Roll into a 6" x 12" rectangle. Cut the rectangle in half lengthwise and cut into 3" strips. Tie each strip into a knot and bake at 400°F for 15 minutes.

5. Process garlic and oil in food processor. Toss hot bread knots with this mixture. Add salt and cheese and serve.

Long Island Wine

John and Lois Ross
Proprietors
Ross' North Fork Restaurant

126

Long Island Wine

In a saturated world market where one can buy any kind of wine at any price, why buy Long Island wine? You should buy Long Island wine for one reason: to increase the enjoyment of your dining experience. Every bottle of local wine contains more than fermented grape juice in a fancy bottle. It contains a story. And to know the story, you have to know the people, and you have to visit the winery. Suddenly, you will be sitting at dinner with friends and family explaining to them how this wine was made, why this vintage was a good one for this varietal, and why it is the perfect wine for this occasion.

We are very fortunate to live in the midst of a quality wine region. It's like living near the vineyards of Alsace — the people there are very proud of what they have. It's no different on the North Fork.

Personal experience with the wine community has been one of my life's great enjoyments. When I open a bottle of Long Island wine and serve it with a crisp Long Island duck, a special chemistry takes place — and a story emerges.

Wine as a Beverage

Wine is a beverage that has a special affinity to food because it is food. On the North Fork, we grow some of the best food in the world and we are fortunate to have high quality wine to complement it.

There are basically three ways that we use wine with food: as a cooking medium; in a sauce or marinade; and as a beverage to drink with food. They are all important and can signficantly enhance the dining experience when used properly.

Wine as a Cooking Medium

Cooking food in wine has been practiced for centuries. It adds acidity, flavor, and complexity to a dish. Common examples are sole vin blanc, beef burgundy, and chicken coq au vin. When cooking with wine, you usually add it at the beginning, boiling off the alcohol and reducing it to a concentrated liquid. Because of this you should use good quality wine when cooking. It doesn't have to be expensive but it should be good enough to drink. The flavors contributed by the wine to a cooked dish are subtle and difficult to indentify, but they give the finished product a new dimension.

Wine in a Sauce or Marinade

White wine sauce, beurre blanc and bordelaise sauce are classic examples of wine in a sauce. Grilled leg of lamb marinated in a red wine and rosemary is an example of a marinade. Simply cooked foods such as chicken breast, salmon fillet, or steak are greatly enhanced by a sauce or marinade. Most recipes combine a meat, poultry or fish stock with wine, herbs, and a thickening agent. Sauce cookery is at the heart of a chef's skill.

Wine as a Beverage with Food

There has been much written on pairing wine with food. I can say, with authority, that a meal without wine is like a day without sunshine. Beyond that the rules can be complex and confusing. The most important rule is to rely on your judgment and your own sense of enjoyment. It's also important to realize that you need people to enjoy food and wine. That's why a wine bottle is 750 ml., so four people can enjoy the conviviality of it together.

If you dine with several people, it's best to have more than one wine. Start with a white and move to a red. Or start with a light, young wine and move to a full bodied wine — in the same way you start with a seafood dish and move to meat or poultry. Or you begin with a light appetizer and finish with a richer entree.

The weight of a wine (or food) is probably more important than the color. Usually a wine with a high alcohol content, barrel fermentation, and some aging will be "heavier" than one without. Good quality light wines have a fresh fruit aroma, lively acidity, and a light texture. They complement similar foods, such as flounder, oysters on the half shell and grilled chicken breast. As the fat content and complexity of a food increases, the weight of the wine should increase.

When a chef enhances a dish with herbs, spices, marinades and sauces it becomes more flavorful and often requires a more flavorful wine. Chicken teriyaki or shrimp and mussels with apples and curry might go with a gewurztraminer or voignier. A roast duck with plum sauce would go with a merlot.

Finally, the traditional guidelines of serving white wines with seafood, red wine with meat, young before old, light before full-bodied, dry before sweet, and inexpensive before expensive are useful but not too important. Your common sense and desire to create a delicious meal will serve you well.

Note: I have included some wine recommendations with my recipes as a personal suggestion — they are only that.

John Ross and Alex Hargrave, HARGRAVE VINEYARDS

Charles Massoud, PAUMANOK VINEYARDS

Kip Bedell
BEDELL CELLARS

Eric Fry
LENZ WINERY

The Ross
Family

L-R., Helen, John, Sarah,
Lois, & Stewart.

L-R., Lois, Sharon, Sanford, & John.

Owning and operating Ross' North Fork Restaurant has been a family project from the beginning. Our family life existed in and around the restaurant. Although none of our children ever had any intention of becoming restaurateurs, they all contributed immensely to the success of the operation. My wife Lois, whose heart really rests with her music, worked faithfully as hostess, bartender, bookeeper and training director. Our employees became our extended family as we spent so many holidays and weekends together. For me, going to the restaurant every day wasn't really work. I couldn't wait to get my hands on the food.

— John C. Ross

PART TWO

RESTAURANT
"GRAVEYARD"

*Historical anecdotes and fond memories of
North Fork Restaurants, past and present*

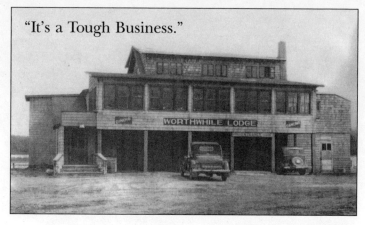

"It's a Tough Business."

The Worthwhile Lodge on the Sound in Southold.
A former speakeasy became a restaurant owned by Bill Worth
in the 1930's, and a popular place for young couples to dance.

Two a.m. and you've been
On your feet since noon.
Open for lunch. Open for dinner.
Open for late supper too.

Seven days a week. Eighteen hours a day.
Three hundred sixty five days a year.
The delivery truck is late. Your party of twelve is early.

Punching in. Punching out.
A waiter calls in sick.
A smile on your face when your feet are frowning.

"Can we have that table in the corner?"
A dozen cheerful waiters singing
Happy Birthday to Grandma.

Soup du jour is onion. You've just
run out of onions.
Medium rare. Well done. Over easy.

Somebody orders the soup du jour.
You've got to love this business
to be in it.

      – *Anonymous*

INTRODUCTION

It is my hope that these pictures, names and dates bring back memories to those who have enjoyed the restaurants of the North Fork over the years. But I especially want to honor the restaurant owners and their employees: from the 14-year-old busperson to the high school waitress to the recent immigrant; to the personable bartender; to the accommodating host; to the temperamental chef; to the stressed-out owner. In addition to their hard, often thankless work over every weekend and holiday and under the most difficult working conditions, they have made a priceless contribution to the character and personality of the North Fork. I think they are very special people.

Because of extensive media coverage, high real estate values, a newfound wine industry, and a proliferation of excellent restaurants, we sense that the beautiful North Fork has just been discovered. But it just isn't true. In 1905 there were two 100-room hotels in South Jamesport, another 100-room hotel in Orient and many smaller ones in between. Before that Greenport was a booming whaling town, a shipbuilding town, and one of the busiest oyster towns in the country. During prohibition, the North Fork was a busy place (not in a way that people can talk specifically about), and World War II brought shipbuilding to the forefront again. After the war, the family automobile changed our lifestyles forever. The proliferation of restaurants parallels the proliferation of cars. We needed a destination and we were hungry when we got there. It still continues today.

Every Spring, new restaurants sprout up on the North Fork like wild mushrooms. The earthy aromas, unusual shapes and exotic flavors tantalize owners and followers alike, but unless extreme caution is shown, backed up by intense knowledge, the result can be poisonous.

The formula for a successful restaurant is to find a good location, create delicious food, and provide friendly service within a beautiful atmosphere.

The North Fork of Long Island attracts people with its rural charm and rich history. The abundance of fresh fruits and vegetables, local ducks, and delicious seafood is poetry to a seasoned foodie. The emergence of our own distinctive wines has transformed a rural farm area into a culinary region. Unique individuals contribute to a cosmopolitan atmosphere, making the North Fork a seductive destination. And the perceived casual life style is a breath of fresh air to stressed-out commuters. The North Fork is like a fairyland at the end of the expressway.

The men and women who participate in this drama make a great contribution. They pour their hearts and souls into making their operations survive. In the end they all create a beautiful fabric that is the center of entertainment for its residents. The reviews, the ads, the stories and the gossip all provide a never-ending source of excitement in the community. Because of this, the restaurants of the North Fork are one of its greatest treasures, capturing the unique personality of the area, while providing people with good food and companionship.

But this is the romantic side of it. The reality is that many restaurants fail after a season or two. The reasons include a short season with erratic volume, heavy competition, long hours over weekends and holidays, and never ending personnel problems. North Fork customers are very sophisticated diners. They know New York City restaurants, Nassau County reastaurants, and South Fork restaurants. Their expectations are high, but when on the North Fork, they expect (and get) lower prices and usually a more "casual" experience.

Restaurant owners are prey to all sorts of people and institutions that support and feed off them: purveyors, banks, insurance agencies, the health department, the liquor authority, the sales tax bureau, the labor department, sales reps of all kinds, groups seeking donations, fire inspectors and of course food critics. They are also the victims of unruly customers and ax grinders who probably have no one left to pick on.

So why do they do it? Is it in their blood? Perhaps they are a little crazy and just can't function in a more structured environment. Fortunately, many local restaurants rise above all the grim statistics and succeed — both artistically and financially. In the following pages we will look at snapshots of North Fork restaurants over the years and enjoy the memories that they so unselfishly created for us.

Greenport, East Marion and Orient

The historic village of Greenport has its own culture. Its many restaurants over the years reflect the personality of a place that has been home to whalers, yachtsmen, bootleggers, fishermen and farmers.

The rich history of the North Fork is personified by Claudio's. Opened in 1870 by Manuel Claudio, it is still operated by the family, and is the oldest restaurant under continuous management in America.

In the spring of 1990, Claudio's ownership passed to fifth generation family members Bill Jr., sisters Kathy and Beatrice, brother-in-law Jerry and Bill's wife Janice. They expanded Claudio's and the surrounding marina into a major tourist destination that became the centerpiece of a revitalized Greenport. In addition to the classic Claudio's Restaurant and Marina they added a wharf clam bar, a take-out seafood restaurant, a gift shop and a shirt shack. The clam bar became a phenomenal success, capturing a spectacular view of the harbor with live entertainment and casual food.

Claudio's Restaurant is a living museum. The mahogany bar with marble handrails and beveled mirrors backed by etched glass take you back to the 1800's. The menu reflects modern tastes but includes recipes that have been North Fork favorites for decades: baked stuffed clams, New England and Manhattan chowder, oysters on the half shell, steamed lobster and a favorite of the 1950's — lobster thermidor. Flounder in many variations, swordfish, salmon and shrimp are also very popular. North Fork wines are now featured on the wine list.

The Claudio's involvement in the Maritime Festival, the Tall Ships, and other destination events have resulted in a major contribution to the North Fork community.

In 1903 William Pelletreau published *A History of Long Island*, from which we take this photo and excerpt:

"Manuel Claudio, a prominent and respected citizen of Greenport, was born at Fayal on the Azores Islands, December 25, 1839, his parents being Joseph and Mary Claudio. Mr. Claudio's ancestors for several generations were natives of the Azores, the family having originally come from Portugal. His father, Joseph Claudio, was a customs house officer at Fayal, where he died at the age of ninety-seven. In the paternal family were fifteen children, of whom Manuel was the only one who became a citizen of the United States.

"He continued at his native place until the age of twelve, and then went to sea. He was engaged for six years on whaling vessels, making two voyages to the Arctic regions. He was then for some thirteen years connected with the merchant marine, visiting in that time every portion of the globe.

"Mr. Claudio's first visit to Greenport was made in 1856, on the whaling bark Neve, which was owned by Greenport people. In 1870, after retiring from the seas, he decided to make that village his home, and established himself in the hotel [and restaurant] business there. In this enterprise, which he still continues, he has enjoyed marked success, and he is one of the best known and most substantial old citizens of Greenport and that section. Mr. Claudio has always taken an active interest in the affairs of the community, and he is among the leading and influential men of the Democratic party in Greenport.

"He was married in 1868, and has two sons, Frank J. and William, both of whom are well known young men of Greenport. His eldest son, Frank J. Claudio, is also successfully engaged in the hotel business in that village."

The Lewis Publishing Company, 1903

138

Mitchell's Restaurant, Hotel, and Marina
Now the site of Mitchell Park

Front Street
Greenport

Harry Mitchell opened Mitchell's in the middle of the Great Depression, in 1933. It grew to 500 seats, a famous rectangular bar, a hotel, and a marina. Harry and his wife Pauline operated it until 1972. The restaurant was destroyed in a fire in 1978.

During World War II, Mitchell's was open 24 hours a day to take care of shipbuilding crews in Greenport. All food was cooked on coal fired stoves. The big ovens reached 500 degrees and could cook 16 lobsters at once on steel racks. A heavy flat top grill was placed over the burners to cook steaks and chops. Harry's son Arnold joined Henry Buerkle as chef after the war.

The menu, heavy on seafood, changed little over the years. Lobster was very popular but, unlike today, rarely steamed. It was baked in those ovens, often with a stuffing. Flounder almondine was a staple, along with striped bass, bluefish, weakfish, cod and sword. Lobster thermidor and newburg were specialties of the house. The menu was filled out with prime rib of beef, steak, lamb chops, Long Island duck, roast turkey, and baked ham. Shellfish included fried shrimp, Peconic Bay scallops and oysters. Complete dinner prices ranged from $4.50 to $7.50 in the 1960's.

Many people considered Mitchell's to be the premiere restaurant on the North Fork during the '40s, '50s and '60s. In forty years of continuous operation it was a major influence on the social life of the North Fork.

Harry Mitchell
Owner of Mitchell's Restaurant, Hotel and Marina

Postcards of Mitchell's Dining Room,
Greenport Harbor, and
the famous Rectangular Bar

141

OPEN FOR BREAKFAST

8 A. M.

OUR SPECIALTY

PECONIC BAY SCALLOPS

MITCHELL'S
DINNER DE LUXE

Celery and Olives

APPETIZERS

Chopped Chicken Livers .50 Extra	Clams on Half Shell .50 Extra		Herring Fillet in Cream Sauce .50 Extra
Tomato Juice Cocktail	Melon		Fruit Cocktail
V – 8 Juice		Pineapple Juice	
Shrimp Cocktail .75 Extra	Stuffed Clam .75 Extra		Lobster or Crab Meat 1.00 Extra
Oysters on Half Shell	1.00 Extra (In Season)		

SOUPS

Manhattan Clam Chowder

Soup Du Jour

Price of Entree Denotes the Price of Complete Dinner

ENTREES

Tenderloin or Sirloin Steak 7.50	* Fried Peconic Bay Scallops 4.75
Roast Prime Ribs of Beef 6.50	Broiled Blue Fish 4.50
Broiled Lamb Chops 6.00	Fillet of Flounder Saute 4.50
Breaded Veal Cutlet, Tomato Sauce 5.50	Fillet of Flounder Almondine 5.00
Veal Parmagiana 6.00	Fillet of Flounder.................................... 5.50
Broiled Chopped Steak, Saute Onions 4.75	Poached with Lobster Newburg Sauce
Baked Virginia Ham, Pineapple Ring 4.50	Crab Meat Au Gratin 6.00
Roast Vermont Turkey 4.50	* Soft Shell Crabs on Toast, Tartar Sauce ... 5.75
Half Roast Long Island Duck, ½ Duck 5.50	* Fried Shrimp... 5.00
Roast Chicken, Sat. & Sun. 4.50	Lobster Meat Cakes 6.25
Half Broiled Chicken 4.50	Lobster Thermidor 6.25
Chicken a la King 4.50	Lobster a la Newburg 5.75
	Broiled Lobster Tails 8.00

Fried Oysters 5.50

Sauteed or Broiled .50 Extra

Extra Plate Service Charge .50

No Substitutes

Coffee — Tea — Milk — Choice of Dessert

We Use Hampton Half and Half

Menu – 1968

Orient Point Inn

Located
across from the
Cross Sound
Ferry

1785 - 1972

Orient Point House, Orient Point,
Suffolk County, Long Island
M.B. Parsons, Proprietor

"**A**s more and more tourists came from the city, the wealthy and upper middle class tourists began to travel farther and farther east to escape the crowds at the large resorts. By the 1870's, smaller hotels such as the Greenport House, Clarke House, Booth House, and the Orient Point Inn were becoming the vacation destination for the well-to-do politicians, artists, writers, hunters, and fisherman from up and down the east coast of the country."

Arnold Mitchell gave the Orient Point Inn its last revival in the mid-1960's. As you can see by this quote from the *Traveler Watchman*, written by Amy Folk, the North Fork has been a tourist destination for a long time. In the late 1800's travel was by train and steamboat. After the turn of the century, the automobile began its ascendancy and later came to transform our lives.

Shore
ON THE *Dinner*
TERRACE
$5.50

BAKED STUFFED CLAMS
CLAM BISQUE or SOUP DE JOUR
HOT ROLLS-COUNTRY BUTTER
GLASS OF SAUTERNE
BROILED LOCAL LOBSTER
STUFFED WITH CRABMEAT
DRAWN BUTTER
CHOICE OF SALAD
ICE CREAM   COFFEE

FAMOUS FOR
INTERNATIONAL DISHES
LUNCHEON $1.50 UP

FOR RESERVATIONS CALL ORient 2-0111

ARNOLD'S
INN and HOTEL
End Route 25   Orient Point, L. I.
CLOSED EVERY WEDNESDAY

143

The Shady Lady
La Cucina
Porky's

Route 48
Greenport

For over 45 years this building was known as Porky's Restaurant. "Porky" was actually Walter Sledjeski, the son of a Polish potato farmer and a self-made entrepreneur. Between 1950 and 1980 Walter and his wife Sophie ran one of the most successful restaurants on the North Fork. The large portions of simple but delicious food and the warm service supported the slogan, "gracious country dining." With his good humor, soft heart, and stubborn in-your-face personality, Porky had many regular customers and catered parties for volunteer firemen, the Rotary Club and many others.

Porky's restaurant career began in 1939 when he leased a small bar and marina in Southold where the Mill Creek Inn is located now. He called it the Sea Shell. Many years later Joe Oates built the present Sea Shell across the road. In more recent years, Joe's son-in-law Greg Power and his wife Carol owned the Sea Shell. Porky, wanting to own his own property, bought a beautiful old house on the North Road in Greenport and converted it into a restaurant. It opened on April 1, 1950 as "Porky's."

After Walter Sledjeski died in 1983, his son Richie ran the business until 1996. He then leased it in 1997 to Bruce Stewart, who opened "La Cucina." In 1998 Bobbie Zorn bought the property and completely renovated it into "The Shady Lady."

"Porky" Walter Sledjeski circa 1939

The Sea Shell Inn circa 1941

The Townsend
Manor Inn

Main Street
Greenport

A handful of North Fork restaurants have operated for years without a change of concept or of owners. The Townsend Manor started out as the private home of whaling captain George Cogswell in 1835. Lillian Cook Townsend bought it in 1926 and turned it into "Ye Olde Townsend Manor Inn." The Gonzalez family took over in 1954 and has operated it ever since.

The Townsend Manor Inn is now a resort, occupying a beautiful property on Stirling Harbor complete with guest rooms, a swimming pool, docking facilities, and a restaurant. The restaurant serves traditional recipes and has always been known for its planked fisherman's platters.

The Coronet

Front Street and Main
Greenport

Some locations were destined to become coffee shops. This busiest of all corners on the North Fork is one of those locations. Open at 4 a.m. for the fishermen, serving the venerable coffee club of local businessmen and politicians at 8 a.m., (their motto was "often in error but never in doubt"), and handling hordes of tourists the rest of the day — the Coronet and its owner, Gary Ostroski, saw a slice of life that few others see. Gary, who started working at the Coronet in 1972 and bought it in 1981, has the kind of mellow personality and friendly demeanor that can handle such a life. The Coronet was originally opened in 1946 by John and Alexandria Drossos. It was subsequently owned by Steve Macros, Marilyn Lang, and Jerry King. The old soda fountain appearance and 1950's architecture have made it a Greenport landmark. Its welcoming presence on Greenport's busiest corner has become a symbol of the North Fork and its rural charm.

147

Newsday Photos by Paul Bereswill

Greenport's Great Toilet War is centered on the Coronet Coffee Shop, in foreground above, with the mayor's office, at 216 Main St., a prominent battle site. The sign of the times, photo above left, hangs on the coffee shop door.

We do not have public toilet. Please see the Mayor at 216 Main St. or go to the Village Hall on 3rd Street for assistance. Thank You. Our bathrooms are for our customers.

The Coronet "toilet wars"

148

Bruce's
Cheese Emporium
and Café

Main Street
Greenport

S ituated on one of the prime corners of the North Fork, Main Street and Front Street in Greenport, Bruce Bollman's Cheese Emporium and Café has introduced gourmet food to a lot of people. Along the way his friendly, easygoing personality has captured all the locals and many tourists.

Bruce was born in Queens, but has spent time on the North Fork since childhood. He graduated from New York City Community College, majoring in hotel/restaurant management, and went to work for Vincent Sardi at the famous Sardi's Restaurant. Starting as a doorman, he worked every position over five years, ending up as general manager. After a two-year stint with the old Schrafft's chain, he settled down in Greenport, opening his own very small store called The Cheese Emporium. The year was 1974. Until Bruce came along, we could only get cheddar and Velveeta on the North Fork. He introduced French bread, extra virgin olive oil, holiday gift baskets, gourmet coffee and homemade fudge. He moved twice, ending up on the corner in Greenport serving lunch including local wine and beer. The "little cheese shop" was looking more and more like a restaurant. After more than thirty years, Bruce's is now a North Fork institution.

The Rhumb Line Restaurant
Bill Worth's Restaurant
The Hotel Greenport
Steve's Vienna Restaurant and Hotel

Route 25
Greenport

In a building that was once an elegant private home of the late 1800's, the Rhumb Line began as Steve's Vienna Restaurant and Hotel. It was owned by Austrian-born Stephan Cvija and was one of the most elegant restaurants in Greenport during the booming oyster and shipbuilding years of the early 1900's.

Bob and Carol Copas bought the building and turned it into the Rhumb Line in 1974. Bob was a sailboat enthusiast, a Porsche driver and a restaurateur with lots of personality. The Rhumb Line had a long, successful run as a pub style restaurant that did excellent volume — even in the winter. It featured almost every kind of imported beer along with good chowder, burgers, and seafood. Its walls were decorated with all kinds of nautical memorabilia. After Bob retired, his daughter Jackie managed the restaurant until it was sold about 2001.

The Kitchen
Portobello Restaurant
Phil's Sports Bar
Billy's Bistro
Catch of the Day
Grinn's
Brian's Song
Terrace East
Kraus' Snack Bar

Route 25
Greenport

T his building on Route 25 just west of the Village of Greenport has had nine tenants in the past forty years. It has nice location, with visibility, parking, and an attractive setting. In part, the turnover reflects the difficulty of operating a restaurant in a seasonal resort area. Any owner faces intense competition, a long off season and high operating costs.

By far the most successful and long-lasting tenant was Brian Kavanagh. He opened his Irish pub style restaurant in 1975 and called it "Brian's Song." He developed a large local following and became famous for his St. Patrick's Day celebrations where he served corned beef and cabbage, Irish beer, and even painted the highway with green shamrocks. It was a friendly restaurant with a casual menu. Brian knows of at least eighteen people who met at his restaurant and went on to get married. Brian is definitely an "old school" North Fork chef who had experience at Porky's, Mitchell's and Cliff's Elbow Room, among others, prior to opening his own place. Brian's Song was sold in 1988.

Matthew Murphy, chef owner of Antares, has operated The Kitchen as a casual comfort food alternative to his fine dining restaurant in Antares Brewer Yacht Basin.

Kraus' Snack Bar, 1960's

SNACK BAR
CHARBROILED

Coca-Cola CHARCOAL HOUSE

Brian's Song
Restaurant

Dear customers -
Welcome! Our goal here at Brian's is to
present the finest of quality food, drink and
service. Together with my crew, we wish
you a most pleasant and enjoyable
evening and hope to see you again soon... Brian

· appetizers ·

baked clams 1.50

clam chowder .75

shrimp cocktail 2.50

fruit cocktail .50

creamed herring filets 1.25

tomato juice w/ lime .50

french onion soup au gratin 1.00

· entrees ·

5.95 fresh broiled flounder
5.95 fresh broiled bluefish
5.95 fresh broiled striped bass
.50 deep fried flounder tempura
6.95 baked stuffed flounder
7.25 deep fried shrimp O'Brian
7.50 shrimp scampi
6.25 shrimp salad plate
8.25 jumbo lamb chops
6.25 broiled red snapper

baked clam dinner 4.75
chopped steak 5.25
sm. sirloin steak 5.50
lg. sirloin steak (plain or marinated) 7.95
soft shell crabs 7.25
crab 'n' turf 8.50
shrimp 'n' steak 9.25
broiled filet mignon 8.95
Brian's pizzle platter 5.25

above served w/ baked potato or french fries or rice pilaf
salad (choice of dressing)
bleu cheese .25 ex sour cream .15 ex

· desserts and beverages ·

.75 ice cream   rice pudding .75

1.25 cheesecake   hot deep dish apple crumb cake .75

1.25 parfait cherry/choc/de menthe   coffee or tea .50

.75 milk   irish coffee O'Brian 1.50

carafe of wine 2.50

Menu from
Brian's Song,
1980's

Drossos
Stantons Night Club

Route 25
Greenport

Nick and Pat Drossos opened Drossos Restaurant in the 1960's. Nick's parents, John and Alexandria, had a large house located on Route 25 in front of the present day motel. They ran it as a tourist home. In 1951, they built the motel and opened a small snack bar and miniature golf course. Their tourist home burned down in 1963 but the motel was saved.

Nick Drossos died in 1974 and his wife Pat continued running the restaurant until the early 1990's. Behind the restaurant she opened a night club called Stantons. It featured DJ's, dancing and entertainment such as the Las Vegas Revue. Pat died in 2003. After the restaurant closed, it became a gift shop.

Scrimshaw

Preston's Dock
Greenport

Rosa Ross (*no relation*) is the chef owner of Scrimshaw, a waterside restaurant. It is literally on the dock at Preston's. Rosa has a rich international background which began in Hong Kong, where she grew up. She moved to England and Italy before coming to the U.S. Her professional career began at the Peter Kump Cooking School (now the Institute of Culinary Education) in Manhattan. Since then, she has been a cooking teacher and author of three cookbooks.

Rosa has had a home in East Marion since 1988. She sincerely hopes to be part of the current revitalization of downtown Greenport, making it a serious culinary destination.

Bay and Main
Bootleggers
Kati's
The Cinnamon Tree
Jacob's Larder

Stirling Square
Greenport

In the mid 1970's we began to see the influence of New York City on the North Fork. Doug Jacobs of Scrimshaw Jewelry fame and French-born chef Robert Hascoat from New York teamed up to open Jacob's Larder in Greenport. The restaurant received a four chef's hat rating from Newsday food critic Barbara Rader and reservations were immediately necessary. Jacob's Larder served imaginative cuisine in an eclectic setting at a time when people were tiring of prime rib, iceberg lettuce, and fried fish. Suddenly we had bouillabaisse and angel hair pasta. Jacob's Larder also featured the Cecil Young Trio for entertainment. During this same period restaurants such as Bonnies by the Bay, La Gazelle, Ross' North Fork, and the Seafarer emerged to offer new competition to the older restaurants.

Jacob's Larder only lasted a year or two. It was purchased by Mae Watson, who opened the Cinnamon Tree. She had a long successful run with an imaginative casual menu, entertainment, and off-premises catering.

Aldo's

Front Street
Greenport

Aldo's Too

Front Street
Greenport

O ver the past 25 years Aldo has been the most purely talented chef on the North Fork. His breads, biscotti, cakes, roasted coffee, and catered specialty foods are the best. He is also one of the kindest, friendliest persons you will find in the community. He is admittedly eccentric, erratic, and a poor businessman.

Born in Sicily, Aldo grew up in the Rhone Valley of France, and opened a small restaurant outside of Nice in a medieval village in the mid-1970's. It's a long story, but he wound up in Greenport in 1979 and has lived on the North Fork ever since. After stints as a waiter and a caterer, Aldo opened his own food store/restaurant in Greenport in 1986. His biscotti has become his biggest success after it was discovered by Manhattan retailer Dean and Deluca. He was also the first one on Long Island to roast his own coffee beans. He is now an institution on the North Fork and one of its most likeable and colorful characters.

The Chowder Pot Pub
The Clam Bar

Third Street
Greenport

B ack in 1976, two doctors liked the view of the Greenport Harbor and Shelter Island from a little spot called the Clam Bar on Third Street by the ferry. So they purchased the property and renovated much of it themselves, using beautiful lumber from a sawmill in Vermont. It opened as the Chowder Pot Pub in 1978 and rapidly developed into more of a restaurant than a pub because of its good food. Culinary Institute graduate Dean Eichorn became a partner with Dr. James Dubovick in 1982 and has remained the manager ever since. A deck and gazebo were added on so that guests could enjoy the magnificent view. The Chowder Pot became a popular place for locals and tourists who enjoyed their prime rib, mussel and clam chowders, and fresh fish. After 27 years of year-round operation it has become a Greenport institution.

The Sterlington Hotel
Meson Olé

Third Street
Greenport

The Hotel Wyandank

The Sterlington Hotel has been around a long time. It used to be right next to the Hotel Wyandank. From about 1948 to 1970, it was operated by Charlie Lellman. The first floor was a bar with light food. In 1988, the chain restaurant franchise Meson Olé opened. It was the first Mexican restaurant in Greenport, and it still operates today.

Meson Olé
The Sterlington Hotel

The Frisky Oyster
Gene's Dockside Inn
Paradise Sweets

Front Street
Greenport

Dennis McDermott and Hank Tomashevski had a weekend home on the North Fork for ten years, but after September 11, 2001, they decided to stay full time. Hank's experience as a chef and Dennis' front of the house skills, plus their combined love of food and wine, motivated them to open The Frisky Oyster. (The name was not chosen to reflect a specialized menu or focus, but it is appropriate since Greenport used to be the commercial leader of the oyster industry.)

The restaurant is small and unassuming, nestled among the stores on Front street. But Dennis is a person who takes every detail of the dining experience very seriously, from the way you answer the telephone to the immaculate condition of the rest rooms.

The menu is compact, easily fitting onto one page. It is written daily, with each ingredient assuming equal weight (loin of lamb, Mainor's Gnocchi, broccoli rabe, wild mushroom sauce). The wine list is similar, reflecting the personal taste of the owners. The customer senses the excitement and realizes this is a place for serious food and wine. Open for only three years, The Frisky Oyster represents a new generation of fine dining restaurants aimed at a sophisticated North Fork customer. This historic building on Front Street began as the Paradise Sweets Ice Cream Parlor, opened in 1923 by George Mellas.

The Fifth Season
Hans Gasthaus
Mac Sea Restaurant

Front Street
Greenport

This space in a storefront on Front Street in Greenport has had many incarnations in recent years. Most of them have been short-lived. But Greenport has undergone a remarkable transformation along Front Street. The beauty of the harbor is captured in Mitchell Park with the carousel and the ice rink; two first class hotels invite overnight guests; old restaurants like the Rhumb Line have been renovated; and new upscale additions like the Frisky Oyster and the Fifth Season have come to town. It looks a little like Sag Harbor's restaurant row. Today Greenport is not just a quaint waterfront town but a dining destination.

Erik and Jennifer Orlowksi appear well qualified to enter this intense competitive environment. Erik is a professional chef who graduated from the New York Restaurant School, has had corporate food service experience, and has excelled in fine dining restaurants. Jennifer is a teacher who grew up in a restaurant family. The Fifth Season is a study in simplicity. There is no bar — they have a beer and wine license and feature only Long Island wine. The kitchen is open, separated from the dining room by a counter. The dining area is small and the menu consists of five first courses followed by five second courses followed by five desserts. Is that why it is called the Fifth Season?

Salamander General Store and Gourmet Food Shop

First Street
Greenport

Salamander Cafe
Brewer Yacht Basin

Claudia Helinski was a serious Foodie who didn't come up through the professional food service ranks; she just loved to cook. After working at the Greenport Tea Company, she and her husband Steve opened the Salamander Cafe in the Brewer Yacht Basin in Greenport. The space was meant to be a snack bar, but the Helinskis turned it into a very innovative, upscale cafe. They catered to boaters, but also developed a strong local following. Claudia began doing off-premise catering at the wineries and at local homes, and in 1997 opened the General Store on First Street in downtown Greenport. She sold the cafe to Matthew Murphy, who turned it into Antares Restaurant.

Front Street
Greenport

Front Street Station
Michaels
O'Donnels
O'Mally's
Fabrizio's

Fabrizio's
212 Front St.
(across from Greenport Theatre)
477-2494

We're known for our delicious
food and congenial atmosphere.
Folks come back for seconds of
our hospitality. Why wait?

OPEN Everyday 11 A.M. - 11 P.M.
Sun. 4 - 11

Finest ITALIAN FOOD

Stella Fabrizio
moved a stainless
steel diner from
the South side of
Front Street to
this location
across the
street from
the movie
theater
in the
late
1960's.

Skippers

———

Route 25
Greenport

S kippers began as a very small building that was used as a drop-off station for fresh milk in the 1920's. By 1955, when the golf course next door was completed, it had grown into a snack bar complete with a takeout window. Captain Blackman, who operated an oyster schooner, was the original owner, naming it Skippers. It gradually evolved into a restaurant when Bobby Heaney bought it in 1980 and completely renovated it into a modern restaurant and bar.

Bobby Heaney is a local Greenport man who served in Vietnam, went to college, thought about becoming a lawyer or teacher — and wound up being a restaurant manager at Soundview. It was a natural for him to want his own place. He has now operated Skippers successfully for over 24 years, joining a small but elite group of North Fork restaurant veterans.

Skippers began as a friendly North Fork pub, and as times have changed it has become more food-oriented, with a menu of veal, pasta, steak, and many shrimp and fish specialties.

Hellenic Snack Bar

Main Rd. (Route 25)
East Marion

John Giannaris and Gus Hartofelis opened the Hellenic Snack Bar in 1976. They were responding to the needs of growing Greek communities in Mattituck and East Marion, and serving tourists as well. The property on Route 25 just east of Islands End Golf Course used to be Brown's Cabins with a snack bar out front. In 1983, the Hellenic was expanded into a full service restaurant serving breakfast, lunch and dinner with cocktails, wines and beer. John Giannaris' family still operates the restaurant with his wife Anna, his son George and his wife Maria. George and Maria have two sons, Yianna and Savvas.

The Hellenic Snack Bar is a quality restaurant that has an excellent reputation on the North Fork. Their famous lemonade that is squeezed fresh to order, their Gyros and Souvlaki, and their whole fresh fish have became signatures. The creative wine list features wines from the "motherland" (Greece), wines from the "backyard" (Long Island) and wines from the West Coast. The menu features Greek specialties such as moussaka and pastitio along with broiled whole calamari with cucumber, tomato, and cabbage salad. The authentic Greek cuisine of the Giannaris family has become one of the attractions of the North Fork.

Trattoria
Bistro Blue
Portobello Ristorante
Puerto Verde
The Boathouse
Chappy's

Stirling Harbor Marina
Manhasset Ave
Greenport

the
"BOATHOUSE"
restaurant

Bon Appetit!

chef Robert from the El Morocco Club

Kitchen Open Daily 4 P. M. - 2 a.m.
Continental Cuisine

FOR RESERVATIONS CALL LEON AT 477-2030
At Stirling Harbor Marina · Off Manhasset Ave. Greenport, N.Y.

There are a small group of "marina" restaurants on the North Fork that are surrounded by boats and enjoy a beautiful summertime nautical atmosphere. The setting of this restaurant atop a hill overlooking Stirling Harbor is spectacular. There have been six tenants in the building over the last 40 years representing some exciting cuisine.

Legrant Chapman first opened Chappy's in 1957. He had

worked at the Seal Ship Oyster Plant until the decline of local oyster business in the 1950's. His son John raised Black Angus cattle on the property that is now Peconic Landing. Steaks from those steers ended up at Chappy's.

Puerto Verde was one of the longest tenants, and the first upscale Spanish restaurant on the North Fork. Their tapas, chorizo and paella introduced new excitement to the local menus. Portobello also did well with their Italian menu. They moved from the seasonal marina setting to Route 25, (now The Kitchen) and then to the former Wine Garden on Route 48 in Mattituck. Bistro Blue was an eclectic American bistro. They introduced the first "martini bar" to our area.

Antares Cafe
Salamanders

Brewers Boatyard
Stirling Marina
Manhasset Ave.
Greenport

This small marina restaurant nestled among the boats was first developed by Claudia Helinski, chef owner of Salamanders. She then moved to downtown Greenport and expanded into off-premise catering and gourmet takeout. Matthew Murphy and his wife Kim opened the very upscale Antares Cafe. Matthew has a Manhattan background and is one of the North Fork's most skilled chefs, using local ingredients such as lobster sauteed in ice wine.

He is one of the few local chefs who has been a guest chef at the James Beard House.

Orient by the Sea
Restaurant and Marina
Summer Wind Restaurant

Route 25
Orient

"The North Fork's Last Stop before Portugal (or New London)."

Since 1979, the Haase family has owned and operated Orient by the Sea Restaurant and Marina. According to Bob Haase, it is the best location and the worst location, depending upon the weather. Surrounded by boats, the restaurant features panoramic views of the water. The North Fork's eastern outpost attracts ferry traffic, boaters, tourists and many locals. Maritime clam chowder, striped bass oreganata, stuffed flounder, coconut shrimp, and steamed twin lobsters are signature menu items. They close the restaurant about November first and re-open at the beginning of May.

In the 1950's, the Marina was an attraction for fishermen. There were very few trees and almost no buildings in the area. One ad promoted waterfront lots for $4500 but had a "buy one, get one free" special. Times have changed!

The Weather Theory

The perfect day for a North Fork restaurant is a dining room full of happy customers. They are enjoying the rural ambiance, the friendly service and the delicious food. The staff moves quickly, handling the orders seamlessly. At day's end the register, and tip bucket, are full.

But the perfect day happens infrequently. The season is so short and there's always a new place to try. Price competition is intense with the $9.95 luncheon, the two-fer, and the $29 prix fixe. Everyone is constantly running, on the phone, and on-line. Take-out, drive-thru, supermarket, ready-to-eat and pre-pared dinners from the fish market. Some people even cook at home. How many nights are left for that leisurely dinner at your favorite restaurant?

Then there is the economy. Except for impulse purchases (and there are many), disposable income is hard to come by, what with the mortgage payment, equity payment, car payment, insurance payments, health costs and taxes. The credit cards are maxed out and confidence in the stock market, interest rates and real estate is a little shaky.

Finally there are the charity events held on the prime nights of the summer. I only wish they had one for restaurants.

But if you ask any restaurateur why it was slow last night, you know the answer ... the lousy weather.

Southold

Sound View Restaurant

Route 48
Greenport

Years ago, Jack Levin was told that he was crazy to buy property on the edge of the Sound. Anything he built would be washed into the sea. So he built the Sound Shore Motel in 1953 and in 1968 bought the Sound View Restaurant from Joe Weigand and Ed Speeches. Joe had converted a fishing station into a restaurant in 1949. Both the Restaurant and the Inn are operating today, providing guests with the most spectacular sunsets on Long Island.

Jack Levin's restaurant career began in 1935 with a food concession stand called Jack's Shack, on the town beach. This hamburger stand was so busy that one July 4th he rang up sales of $1,000 in a single day — from selling burgers at 15¢ apiece! The Sound View Restaurant is now a North Fork institution that epitomizes the beauty of the Sound and a long tradition of North Fork dining. Jack's children, Andrew, Ellen, Jody and Rachel, have all been involved in managing the growing business. Rachel is the current restaurant manager with a lot of help from Ellen.

The menu features lots of lobster, shrimp, fish and clam chowder. Steaks, roast beef, and Long Island duck are also popular. The Gold Room is a beautiful, very busy catering addition. The Sound View represents the North Fork's tradition of modestly priced, family-run restaurants.

THE SEAFOOD BARGE AND ITS NEIGHBORS

The Old Barge
The Shipwreck
Armando's Seafood Barge
The Barge

Port of Egypt Restaurant
The Seafood Barge

Pepi's Ristorante Italiano
Club Wave
Baywatch Cafe
Ciccilino's
The Arrow Bar

Crispy Chicken and Fish

W hen you leave the Village of Southold on Route 25, the road goes through a narrow strip of bayfront that commands a spectacular view of wetlands, marinas, and Peconic Bay. This area has been a popular restaurant location for many years and many tenants have occupied the buildings. But the "anchor" of these buildings is one of the most colorful waterfront restaurants on Long Island — what is now called The Old Barge.

In 1948 Captain Carl D. Reiter towed a navy ammunition barge from Boston to Southold. Soon after, he opened a seafood market — "wholesale, retail, fish and oyster house." It grew into a restaurant called the Barge and the Reiter family operated it for twelve years. In 1962, Armando Cappa leased it and called it Armando's Seafood Barge. Armando was famous for the freshness of his seafood and for introducing oversized steamed lobsters to the area. He did huge volume and attracted many tourists to the North Fork. Armando worked in the front with his apron and chef's hat, opening clams on the half shell. Stanley Garren was his chef in the back. He made big kettles of chowder, steamed lobsters, and worked four large deep fryers. On some summer Sundays they would do 1200 customers with 20 waitresses working the floor.

In 1982 Armando had a dispute with Captain Reiter's widow Helen and she did not renew his lease. He then opened a newly renovated restaurant on the old site of the Port of Egypt restaurant next door. The property is owned by the Lieblins. Armando continued to call his restaurant "Armando's Seafood Barge," and Helen Reiter's place became "The Old Barge." The new barge was a beautiful building with great water views and initially was very busy. In 1989 Armando transformed the old Arrow Bar into an upscale Italian restaurant called Ciccilino's. His

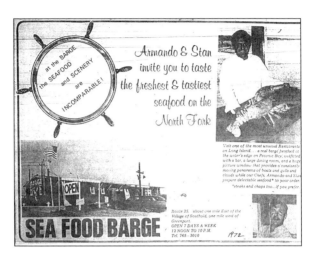

wife Marie was co-owner and manager. At this time Armando also owned a small take-out restaurant by the main road called Crispy Chicken and Fish. But by the early 1990's Armando was developing health problems and emerging from a long economic recession. He was forced to file for bankruptcy in 1993.

Richard Ehrlich took over the Seafood Barge (on the Port of Egypt property) and turned it into a very upscale seafood restaurant with contemporary cuisine and a very good local wine list. He hired top chefs such as Michael Meehan and was rewarded with an excellent *New York Times* review.

In the meantime the Old Barge continued to be owned by the Reiter family and has had several tenants. For a short period it was renamed the Shipwreck. Ciccilino's became Club Wave and the Baywatch Cafe, before its present incarnation as Pepi's Ristorante Italiano. The crispy chicken and fish building has been unoccupied for many years. Probably the stress of managing three restaurants at once caught up with Armando, but at his prime he ran a great operation.

Port of Egypt Restaurant

Main Road
Southold

T he sandy area surrounding "Budds Pond" (the part of
Southold Bay closest to the marina) was a small community in the early 1900's called "Little Egypt" because of
its sandy surroundings. The fishing station in the 1920's where
they rented rowboats was called "Port of Egypt" by its owner.
Much later, when the Lieblein family bought the property in 1946,
they found an old wooden sign with the name Port of Egypt on
it. They decided to re-use the name.

Everyone on the North Fork is familar with Port of Egypt
Marine. They've been in the boat business in Southold since 1946.
What many have forgotten is that the Port of Egypt Restaurant
was in business from 1946 until 1977. While William and Herbert
Lieblein operated the marina, a third brother, Herman Lieblein,
was a chef. The original restaurant, more of a tavern, was down
by the water. It sold beverages and casual food to the fisherman
and tourists who rented boats.

When the inlet was dredged in 1962, they moved the restaurant to where the Seafood Barge is today. The Liebleins expanded
the restaurant, creating a more upscale menu. Herman's Manhattan Clam Chowder was famous, its recipe a family
secret. His seafood and German dishes such as sauerbraten were very popular. Herman's mother was from
Vienna and his German father had once worked at
Lüchow's in New York.

173

The Old Barge

Pepi's Ristorante Italiano

The North Fork Restaurant Evolves

After World War II, dining out at your favorite restaurant grew to become a major source of entertainment. Giving your wife a break, meeting friends, or enjoying the romance were good reasons to get out of the house. For many it became a weekly ritual. And for many years two people could dine out for less than $20, including drinks, tax, and tip. During the period from 1950 to 1980 restaurants such as Mitchell's, Porky's, Soundview, and Claudio's were very busy. Their menus were similar and extensive. Appetizers included fruit cocktail, tomato juice, shrimp cocktail, and half shell clams. Chowder and soup du jour were always present along with a salad of iceberg lettuce and your choice of Italian, French, Russian, or blue cheese (+$.50). The entree page would be headed by the words "From the Sea." Many deep fried items would be followed by shrimp scampi, lobster newburg, broiled lobster, and Catch of the Day. The next page was "From the Land" — roast prime rib, roast turkey, roast duck and baked ham, followed by broiled steak, filet mignon, and lamb chops. Entrees included a baked potato (wrapped in foil) or french fries, and often a side of tired looking vegetables. Desserts included pie (a la mode +$.50), ice cream, cheesecake, and Jell-o. Restaurants began to specialize more: The Seafood Barge and Orient By the Sea became famous for seafood, especially lobster; Cliff's Elbow Room pioneered the marinated steak; Bill Brasby's had a banquet room and served buffets featuring the steamship round; Little Joe's was Italian.

By 1975 a distinct change took place, both nationally and locally. People got serious about food and wine. Julia Child was on T.V. James Beard was writing about cooking in America and Michael Field was editing the Time/Life series of International Cookbooks. Everyone read Craig Claiborne and Pierre Franey in *The New York Times.* Food professionals graduated from the Culinary Institute and the Cornell Hotel School. The American chef became a celebrity.

Here on the North Fork some of the old restaurants grew a little tired. Their menus hadn't changed in 25 years. I came to Southold in 1973 and opened Ross' North Fork with the notion that this was the ultimate "backyard."

Everything was right here: fish, shellfish, ducks, outstanding vegetables and fruit — and soon, wine. All you had to do was buy fresh local ingredients in season, cook from scratch, and keep the menu simple. I learned that behind all those local ingredients were people — interesting characters who worked hard and added an exciting dimension to my job.

By the early 1980's there was an ever-growing group to increase restaurant quality and variety. Ethnic restaurants, Nouvelle cuisine, New American cuisine, and regional cuisine. Some were short lived: Jacob's Larder in Greenport, Chinam in Southold, the Old Oyster Factory, and the Mediterranean in Mattituck. Others lasted longer: Bonnies by the Bay in New Suffolk, Larry Mitchell's Seafarer on Kenny's Beach and Puerto Verde at Stirling Marina. And some newcomers survived the test of time: La Gazelle in Southold where French-born chef Robert Hascoat and his vivacious wife Christine attracted many customers to a higher level of cuisine and service; Matt Kar at the Jamesport Country Kitchen increased the quality of casual dining and incorporated local wine into his menu from the beginning. Suddenly the competition was getting intense. Chefs became the focal point, with excellent service and a beautiful ambiance right behind.

Suffolk Times, 1984
"Rookie Chef Steps
up to the Stove"

Joanthony's
Ross' North Fork Restaurant
The Carriage House
Armando's
Jimmy's

Main Road
Southold

In 1954 James Warnaka opened this restaurant, calling it Jimmy's. Mr. Warnaka, a W.W. II veteran, had operated a restaurant in the post office building in Southold Village for seven years when he decided to move East. "It is modernly equipped both in the dining room and kitchen with ample room for table and counter customers. A soda fountain and candy cases add to the attractiveness ... there's lots of room for parking."

After a brief ownership by Armando Cappa (who called it Armando's), Stephen Mutkoski bought it in 1968. He upgraded and enlarged the building, naming it The Carriage House. There was even an old horse-drawn carriage out front. He added a salad bar, a dessert table, and a piano bar. The menu featured chateaubriand, surf n' turf and Peconic Bay scallops. There was a popular business table for lunch where many local merchants met.

Stephen Mutkoski returned to the Cornell Hotel School where he became Professor of Wine Education. He sold the restaurant to recent graduate John Ross. My wife Lois and I moved to Southold in 1973 and opened Ross' North Fork Restaurant. At a time when chain restaurants were multiplying exponentially, I was determined to keep my menu simple, use only fresh ingredients, and cook all products from scratch.

In addition, we featured wine from New York. After operating Ross' in this location for eleven years we moved up to the North Road. After a total renovation of the old Raymond's we re-opened as Ross' North Fork in 1984. It was coincidental that in 1973 Alex and Louisa Hargrave planted grapes in Cutchogue. Our interest in local wines was a natural. Joan and Tony Mannino took over the old Ross' and renamed it Joanthony's. They turned it into a family restaurant where hamburgers were the mainstay of the menu.

THE CARRIAGE HOUSE

Main Road, Southold, New York

Bloody Mary ∽ $1 ∽

Soup 'N Sandwich $1.25

ROAST BEEF
Polish HAM and Swiss CHEESE
ROAST TURKEY
Escorted by — Crunchy Chips, Lettuce and Tomato, Dill Pickle

Each ∼ $1
Two Halves of Any Two ∼ $1
or Three Halves of All Three ∼ $1.50

SHRIMP DELIGHT
Jumbo Shrimp on Crisp Bed of Lettuce
Garnished with Wedges of Egg, Tomato and Lemon,
topped with Remoulade Sauce.
$1.95

D-r-r-r-y Martini ∽ $ .90 ∽

REEF and BEEF
Noonday Cut of Sirloin "As You Like It"
Served with a Petite Lobster Tail
$2.95

Irish Coffee ∽ $1 ∽

YOUR CHOICE
Hot Roast Beef Sandwich
French Fried Jumbo Shrimp
Soft Shell Crab on Toast
Served with French Fries, Lettuce and Tomato
$1.50

PORK CUTLET WITH PAN GRAVY
Served with whipped potato
and applesauce.

$1.40

SANDWICHES

Hamburger	.50	Tuna Salad	.50
Cheeseburger	.55	Fried Fish	.75
Grilled Cheese	.50	Shrimp Salad	.90

DESSERT

Mum's Old Fashioned Cheesecake 60
Freshly Baked Pies 35
Ice Cream 30

BEVERAGES

Coffee .15   Tea .15   Milk .20   Soda .20

THE MOST GENEROUS DRINKS IN TOWN

178

John and Lois Ross

179

O'Mally's
Ross' North Fork
Raymond's
Bill Clay Miller's

North Road, Rt. 48
Southold

T his building on the North Road (Route 48) began in the 1960's as a restaurant/dance club under the ownership of Bill Clay Miller. The bartender was required to play the drums and Bill did the rest. Former Mitchell's chef Ray Pawlik and bartender Ray LaRiviere bought out Bill Clay Miller and turned it into Raymond's Restaurant in 1973. I bought it in 1984 and moved my North Fork restaurant from the Main Road to this location. I sold it in 2000, and it became O'Mally's. It is now owned by Phil Manino, who owns O'Mally's in East Hampton and has operated many area restaurants over the years.

"... There a local winemaker, a chatty vegetable farmer, or a hunch for good food will probably lead you to John Ross and his North Fork Restaurant. More than any chef in the region, Ross has been working steadily to evolve a genuinely local cuisine, based on Long Island's cooking traditions and its now thriving wine industry.

For more than two decades, Ross has been deep in an ongoing 'conversation' with the wine and food producers of this small community, trading ideas and inspiration back and forth. He was there to encourage local farmers to branch out from cabbage and white potatoes into arugula and Yukon Golds. In late summer Ross arranges with his corn farmer to do a picking at the end of the day just for the restaurant – guaranteeing that his steamed corn is less than three hours off the stalk. His commitment to pouring local wines from producers such as Bedell, Hargrave, Paumanok, and Lenz has exposed their bottles of crisp, balanced 'food wines' to countless customers."

Appellation Magazine, 1997

Many North Fork restaurants have developed a
strong following of regular customers
by creating a warm, friendly environment.

A special occasion for Ann and Ted Swanson.

Always a warm smile from
hostess Isobel and waitress Lucia.

Ross' North Fork Restaurant

First Courses

ROBINS ISLAND OYSTERS	Baked in Garlic and Pernod	8 –
	On the Half Shell	8 –
LITTLENECK CLAMS	Baked Casino Style	8 –
	On the Half Shell	8 –
SAUTEED LONG ISLAND DUCK CAKES		7 –
BAKED STUFFED CHERRYSTONE CLAMS		5 –
ESCARGOT EN CASSEROLE		7 –
STEAMED MUSSELS	In White Wine Sauce	7 –
JUMBO SHRIMP COCKTAIL With Two Sauces		8 –
FRESH FRUIT AND CHEESE		6 –
PESTO WITH ROASTED TOMATO AND LINGUINE		7 –

Entrees

Fresh Finfish & Shellfish

SAUTEED FLOUNDER ALMONDINE		18 –
FILET OF TUNA	With Red Wine, Wild Rice and Portabella Mushroom	19 –
SAUTEED SALMON FILLETS	With Japanese Bread Crumbs	19 –
SWORDFISH PICCATA	Sauteed with Capers, Wine, Pasta	19 –
JUMBO SHRIMP	Sauteed with Garlic, Fresh Tomato, Basil and Homemade Fettuccine	20 –
JUMBO SHRIMP	Deep Fried in Ale Batter with Horseradish Marmalade & Shoestring Fries	19 –
LOBSTER ALFREDO	With Homemade Fettuccine, Cream & Parmesan Cheese	21 –

Meat & Poultry

BONELESS ROAST LONG ISLAND DUCK With Long Grain Wild Rice & Plum Sauce		20 –
PECAN BREADED BREAST OF CHICKEN With Sour Cream & Dijon Mustard		18 –
CHARGRILLED NEW YORK STRIP STEAK (18 oz.) With Onion Rings and Shoestring Fries		22 –
GRILLED FILET OF PORK	With Apple, Pear and Ginger Chutney	19 –

Coeur Des Vignes
La Gazelle
The Southold Inn
The Sunrise Inn

Main Road (Rt. 25) Southold

A t the age of 22, Robert Hascoat came from Brittany in France to New York City. In New York he ended up working in the El Morocco restaurant. Through connections there he spent a summer cooking at The Boathouse restaurant in Stirling Marina, Greenport. From this experience he became a partner with Doug Jacobs and Ed Tobia in opening Jacob's Larder restaurant in Stirling Square. It was 1974. Jacob's Larder jumped off to a very successful start. It was a beautiful renovation of a barn. Cecil Young played the piano and Robert prepared great food in the kitchen. Barbara Rader gave it four chef's hats in *Newsday* and Robert's North Fork career was on its way.

He and his wife Christine purchased the old Southold Inn from Dom Zito in 1975 and renamed it La Gazelle. For the next twenty years, they became the premiere French restaurant on the North Fork. Robert's preparation of flounder grenobloise, bouillabaisse, rack of lamb, frog legs and chateaubriand were refreshing to a community used to prime rib and fried flounder. And Christine's vivacious personality and good service created many regular customers. Sadly, Robert died of cancer in 1995 and soon after Christine sold La Gazelle.

In 1997 George, Donna Marie, and Arie Pavlou purchased La Gazelle. They renovated the upstairs rooms into luxury suites, continued the tradition of French cuisine, and renamed it L'Hotel Coeur Des Vignes. Arie, the chef, learned his skills in France and New York. His specialties include game, such as venison, rabbit, and pheasant, and foie gras prepared in many ways. His steamed striped bass and seared sea scallops with pomegranate are seafood specials.

This historic building began its commercial life as The Sunrise Inn. It had a colorful history as tavern, inn, and (some say) bordello.

Chef Robert Hascoat
La Gazelle

Photos by
Judy Arhens

Sea Shell

Main Road (Rt.25)
Southold

The Sea Shell actually began its existence across the street and a little east, in the building that became the Mill Creek Inn. Walter Sledjeski ("Porky") ran the original Sea Shell Inn from 1939 to 1950. Walter's bartender/cook/sometimes violin player Warren Bricchi took over when Porky opened his new restaurant on the North Road.

By 1958, Joe Oates bought out Warren and ran the Sea Shell. Unable to buy the property, he moved across the street and built the present day Sea Shell in 1967. Joe's daughter Carol, who had been a busgirl for the infamous Pauline at Mitchell's, married Greg Power and they went on to buy the Sea Shell in 1973. Carol and Greg, with some help from their four children, operated a successful year-round restaurant for over 20 years. Their original chef, Dean Eichorn, went on to become a partner in the Chowder Pot Pub.

The Sea Shell has always been a popular local restaurant with modest prices. A friendly bar and lots of local seafood have been trademarks. In 1994, the Power family leased the restaurant to Barbara Grigonis.

The Mill Creek Inn
The Half Shell
    Republic
The Brickyard
The Shell
The Sea Shell Inn

Main Road, Southold

This building during the 1940's was the original "Porky's," with a little pink neon pig over the bar door. In more recent times, the most successful tenant of this beautiful waterfront property was Dean Blakie. Opening in the late '70s, his year-round restaurant provided a new level of competition to the old established places like Porky's, Soundview, Mitchell's, and Claudio's. The bar was a predecessor to the modern sports bar, very active, with bar food available. Many local groups had their parties and meetings there, and they were open for lunch and dinner seven days a week, year round.

Dean also operated the Galley Ho and the Tolendal Inn. The "Ho" was a very popular bar on the bay in New Suffolk. Dean expanded the food offerings until it became a very busy lunch and late night destination. He also took over Brasby's Catering Hall Restaurant in Mattituck, renaming it the Tolendal Inn. It was the first attempt on the North Fork at a catering-only facility. They did weddings, senior proms, and many other large scale events.

Journey's Inn
Hollisters
Le Bar
The Tavern

Main Road, Southold

This building was originally a bar called "The Tavern." In the 1950's it was owned by the LaColla family. In 1963, Joe Oates Jr. bought it and ran The Tavern until the early 1970's. It had a brief run as Le Bar before being completely renovated by the Tuminello family into Hollisters — a popular family restaurant known for its shrimp and steak entrees. They also had a soup and pasta bar. In the 1990's, Jean Paul Hascoat leased it from the Tuminellos and renamed it Journey's Inn. J.P. is the son of the late Robert Hascoat, owner of La Gazelle.

Cliff's Elbow East
Cliff and Phil's
    Lobster House
The Beachwood Cafe
The Seafarer
Jack's

End of Kenny's Road
Southold

This building began as a pizza stand and evolved into a bar called Jack's. It was owned by Jack Larson. In the mid-1970's Larry Mitchell, with help from his brother Cliff and father Arnold, opened the Seafarer. They transformed it into an upscale waterside restaurant with great seafood and a sophisticated wine list. It became a very popular restaurant. In 1983, it was sold to Doug Castoldi, who changed the name to the Beachwood Cafe. In 1987, Cliff Saunders, owner of the Elbow Room, bought it. It was originally called Cliff and Phil's Lobster House, but after a fire and subsequent renovation, they renamed it Cliff's Elbow East.

Billy Berliner had worked for and been a friend of Cliff Saunders since he was 13. He became the manager of Elbow East in 1989, and in 1999 he and his sister Katherine bought the property from Cliff.

They have continued the legacy of the Elbow Room with its marinated porterhouse steaks, stuffed clams and homemade chowder. They offer a lot of specials to fill out the menu and have become a very popular restaurant. Although they are down on the beach, they remain open year round.

THE - GOOD - OLD - DAYS

Photo by Glenn Jochum

MAIN EVENT—Manager Bill Berliner (left) and owner Cliff Saunders, with crustaceans, at Cliff's Lobster House Friday.

*Although Cliff's suffered a fire on Sunday, plans are to reopen with largely the same menu.

Pagano's Italian Restaurant
The Curry Club
John's Steakhouse
Mei-Lin Chinese
      Restaurant
Chinam

Main Road
Southold

This old brick building was a Dodge dealership until the late 1960's. In the '70s the building was renovated by Jim Gray as part of the Feather Hill project. It was then leased to three businesswomen — Renee Kaplan, Anne Matthews, and Jane Lander — who adopted a Vietnamese family and opened Chinam. Chinam was Southold's first upscale Asian restaurant. Huynh Van Hue was the chef. He had previously been a chef at a large restaurant in Saigon, the Bhoung Hong. Chinam opened in the Spring of 1976.

In the early 1980's Joseph Hsieh leased the restaurant and turned it into Mei-Lin Chinese restaurant. Joseph was born in China, grew up in Taiwan and emigrated to the United States. In addition to running the restaurant, he was a tax accountant.

In the 1990's the building next became John's Steakhouse, owned by local chef John Anderson. He stayed only for a year, when it became The Curry Club, an Indian concept.

John Pagano, the current tenant, used to be in the old post office next door. He moved into this building in the mid-1990's with his very successful Italian restaurant and pizzeria.

The General Wayne Inn
Cedar Beach Inn

End of Bayview Road
Southold

Who was General Wayne? He was a soldier in the revolutionary war who became known as "Mad Anthony" because of his daring exploits. He was with George Washington at Valley Forge. He didn't come from Southold and he had nothing to do with the General Wayne Inn.

The General Wayne was built in 1784 as a private residence known as the Major Gilbert Horton House. In 1884 it became a hotel which eventually had a golf course. Over the years it has had many owners and has been a speakeasy, a restaurant, and a catering hall.

On a beautiful tree-shrouded property, three winding miles off the main road in Southold, it evokes a sense of mystery and of times past, when the pace of life was a little slower. The romantic possibilities of this old inn have attracted many owners, but it has spent much of its history closed due to the practical problem of being so out of the way, and not actually being on the water.

In the late 1960's, it was owned by a Mr. Quarty and his wife Lola. They featured dancing, dinner and a bar. Perhaps the most ambitious and successful attempt to operate the General Wayne was by the Norkus family. Bob was the owner with his son Greg the chef and Greg's wife Kate, the baker and hostess. In the late 70's they had a sophisticated menu of local fish and shellfish, ducks and prime rib and on-premise baking.

Visitors and local residents of the North Fork would like to see restaurants like the General Wayne succeed because they lend a charm and unique personality to our community. But the artistic qualities always have to exist in a world of practical considerations.

The Willowmere Inn
(known as "Sophie's")

Main Bayview Road
and Peanut Alley
Southold

On Willow Hill, a little ways off the Main Road, there is a bar so obscure that only a secret group of locals know it exists. Surprisingly, it has been a Southold institution since the mid-1930's. The official name of this beautiful neighborhood bar is the Willowmere Inn, but there is no sign, no advertisements, and no website. There is a small neon sign in the window that says "Budweiser." Everyone locally knows the place as Sophie's.

The Willowmere was opened by Benny Manasek in 1936. He moved here from Joe's Tavern on Boisseau Avenue (which now houses the Ink Spot) because his clients had to park out front in plain view of the townspeople. The Willowmere was off the beaten track, with parking in the rear. Sophie Furmankiewicz bought the Willowmere in 1965 after working at Fishermen's Rest for a few years.

Sophie passed away in 2003 at the age of 79. Her daughter Jenny Bienias has helped Sophie for years and is now turning the business over to Sophie's grandson John Koke. He is continuing the tradition of a friendly local bar. There's a pool table in the Main Room ($.25) and three dart boards. There is also a jukebox. Don't expect too many T.V. monitors or an ad for "Karaoke Night!"

The Grateful Deli
Ropin' Roys Steak House
Shelly's
The Quiet Man Inn
The Village Inn
Phil's Tavern

Main Road
Southold

During Colonial times and up to the early 1900's there were taverns and there were inns. Both would serve alcoholic beverages and both would serve food. The tavern evolved into the modern restaurant and the inn into the modern hotel. An establishment serving only alcohol became known as a "bar."

This building began as Phil's Tavern, a neighborhood place serving local farmers and merchants. It evolved into the Village Inn, which by 1970 was a classic local bar featuring a pool table and a jukebox. It went more upscale as the Quiet Man Inn, with an Irish ambiance and live entertainment.

After brief incarnations as Shelly's and Ropin' Roys, it was completely renovated into a modern deli. This reflects the changing times with strict enforcement of D.W.I. laws. The old neighborhood bar has fallen into decline at the same time that take-out food from every source, including delis, has multiplied to keep up with our fast-paced lives.

2004

1940's

North Fork Food
Johnny's Juke Joint
Hubba Hubba
Rick's Seafood Cafe
Pickles

Rt. 48 at Horton's Lane
Southold

A small two-bedroom house becomes a restuarant. Beginning as Pickles in the early 1980's, it was an early attempt
at healthy, upscale takeout. It then became Rick's, specializing in seafood takeout and "the world's best onion rings."
Perhaps both of these concepts were a little ahead of their time.

Pete Ferrigan was the next owner. He had a passion for the
1950's, as exemplified by his beautiful 1950 Ford Coupe. I think
he needed a place to show it — so he opened a '50s-style drive-in
called Hubba Hubba. It was complete with carhops on roller skates
and curb service. Pete retired, sold it to Claudine, who kept the
'50s theme, upgraded the food quality and ran it very successfully as Johnny's Juke Joint. It was then sold and completely renovated into a serious food store called North Fork Food.

Cutchogue and New Suffolk

Fisherman's Rest

Main Road
Cutchogue

The Village of Cutchogue is located in the heart of the North Fork and its historic business district is on the Main Road (Route 25). Many businesses on the North Fork evoke memories of the past and develop a personality of their own — regardless of who the current owner is. Fisherman's is one of these buildings. It opened in 1947 as a tavern catering to local farmers and fisherman. Over the years it expanded, adding a dining room, and more recently a private party room. Its menu has always been casual Italian with a North Fork personality. They're famous for their thin crust pizza. As you pass the Cutchogue Diner, the Deli, Fisherman's and Wickham's Fruit Farm — you know you're in Cutchogue.

Sophie Furmankiewicz (future owner of The Willowmere Inn) worked here from about 1958 to 1963 when the Pumillos owned it. She is said to have contributed the famous thin crusted pizza. Larry Kirk owned it after the Pumillos until 1989, when it was sold to Billy Smith. It is currently owned by Steve Abbott.

The Cutchogue Diner
The North Fork Diner
Al's Diner
Glover's
The Cutchogue Diner

Main Road
Cutchogue

THE NORTH FORK LIFE   1941
GLOVER'S NEW EATATORIUM

W e are very fortunate that some of the restaurants of the past have been preserved in their original state. In a world of fast food and box stores, they set the North Fork apart as a timeless place of beauty. The Cutchogue Diner is one of these historic places that continues to run as a modern business. We have to thank John Touhey who bought it in 1987 and completed an extensive renovation of the aging diner.

Olin Glover opened the Cutchogue Diner in a wooden building in 1933. In 1941, he bought a gleaming stainless steal structure from the Kullman Dining Car Company and attached it to his old building. Mr. Glover sold his diner in 1948 to Al Harker, who developed a reputation as a very good cook.

Between 1965 and 1987, the Cutchogue Diner was owned by a succession of people: Bill Hagen from 1965 to1981; then Diane Slavonik and Jennie Kapustka until 1985; and Dave DeFriest from

1985 to 1987. John Touhey continues as the present owner in this North Fork landmark.

The Farmer Bar
The Wild Goose
The Blue Top

Depot Lane
Cutchogue

In the old days on the North Fork one of the most important social institutions was the neighborhood bar. It's where men (mostly) relaxed after work, talked about the weather and enjoyed each other's company. The Galley Ho, Fishermans Rest, The Village Inn, The Arrow Bar, and The Whiskey Wind are a sampling. But the Blue Top on Depot Lane was a classic. It was known as a farmer's bar (as opposed to a fisherman's bar).

In 1934, Mary Zamber started the Blue Top bar and grill on the east side of Depot Lane. She and her husband Ray ran it, and by 1936 it was so popular that they moved it down the road to a larger place, at the present location. People raved about Mary's clam chowder, weekend visitors dropped in for great sandwiches, farmers relaxed there after a hard day's work, and organizations and families held parties in the side room. During World War II, the Blue Top was where soldiers wrote to let their buddies know they were okay. After the war, GI's tore division patches off their sleeves and proudly hung them around the mirror.

In 1947 Mary Zamber sold the Blue Top to her sister Victoria Bugdin and her husband Joseph. Over the years, the place was sold to other family members, and starting in the 1960s it was owned by Albert "Red" Grohoski and his wife. They sold it in 1998.

In 2000, it reopened as an upscale restaurant called The Wild Goose. Chef/owner Frank Coe and his wife Barbara Sweeney featured specialties such as duck confit, foie gras, roast lamb and wild salmon. It closed after two seasons. It has now re-opened as The Farmer Bar, specializing in Southern barbecue and an old fashioned bar. Dan Reyburn and "pit master" Ron Philipp are the owners.

Mary and Ray Zamber at the bar, New Year's 1943

The Blue Top, Jan. 8,1957

Harpoon Harry's
Gills
St. Trop
Harbor Inn
The Ho
The Galley Ho

Main Street
New Suffolk

During the 1950's, 1960's and 1970's, North Fork restaurants could be very basic: a small kitchen with a broiler and a deep fryer; a rustic bar with a keg of beer on tap; a tiny dining room with wooden floors and no air conditioning; and a spectacular view of the bay with the smell of fish in the air. The Galley Ho was such a place.

Restaurateurs Dean Blakie, Skip Schoenhaur, and more recently, the Raynor family ran a very popular destination for fisherman, boaters, locals, and summer people. It became a North Fork institution. But the simplicity of managing a local tavern in the old days has been replaced by a more complex formula: the public demands amenities such as air conditioning, upscale cuisine, and a bar with multiple video screens; the landlord requires more rent to pay for insurance and property costs; and regulatory agencies such as the health department and fire department are much stricter than in the past. Finding a tenant that can overcome these obstacles in a very seasonal environment is difficult.

Legends
Bonnies by the Bay
Captain Ahab's
The Harbor Inn

New Suffolk
on the bay

In an era of restaurant turnover and an environment where financial success and artistic success are rarely compatible, Legends has excelled. Diane and Denis Harkoff purchased what was Bonnies by the Bay in 1993. They developed the first successful high tech, sports-themed bar on the North Fork, complete with video games, sports memorabilia and the game of the week. Adjacent to the bar, but completely separate, they developed a dining room with a modern international menu and a reputation for high quality food and wine. From their seemingly out of the way location in New Suffolk they manage to remain very busy all year long. Their menu includes familiar items such as local flounder, shrimp scampi, and prime rib. along with grilled wild boar, thai style shrimp, and tuna sashimi.

Bonnies By the Bay

First Street
New Suffolk

I t's a common cliche to say the restaurant business "gets in your blood." Many a successful restaurateur has trouble walking away from it. Elaine Romagnoli came to the North Fork in 1981, seeking the peaceful rural setting that can be so relaxing after the frantic pace of Manhattan. Her next realization was that the North Fork needed an eclectic, trend setting restaurant. Thus, Bonnies By the Bay was born and Elaine's dreams of peaceful summer weekends came to an end.

Susannah Cancro

In 1982, Bonnies was a trend setter and an excellent restaurant. Elaine was the owner of La Petite Femme in Greenwich Village and later, Bonnies on West 3rd street. She also owned a nightclub called Bonnie and Clyde. Her original Chef, Jude Bartlett, and other staff came from the So-Ho Charcuterie. They introduced rare blackened tuna, cajun popcorn, and lobster tacos. The wooden floors of the old Captain Ahab's were painted in brilliant colors. Bonnie's woke up the sleepy North Fork, demonstrating that quality food could be served in an exciting fashion.

Mattituck

The Old Mill Inn

Mattituck Inlet
Mattituck

S amuel Cox, upon returning from the War of 1812, secured permission from the Town of Southold to construct a tidal mill on Mattituck inlet. Five years later the dam, mill and mill gates were completed. The mill was later included in the Library of Congress as a notable "relatively rare engineering structure."

In 1902 the mill was sold because a new steam-powered mill had come to town. It then became a tavern known as The Old Mill. In 1906 the tidal dam was destroyed by a storm and a swivel bridge was installed. Tavern customers often helped to move the bridge for yachts to come in. The bridge was destroyed in 1955.

Because of its seclusion in the inlet, The Old Mill was a popular drop off for rumrunners during Prohibition. There is still a drop door in the kitchen.

A handful of restaurants on the North Fork began as speakeasies and evolved into full service restaurants over the years. But the Old Mill Inn is an historic North Fork treasure that has retained its original character and personality.

Captain Stanley Naugles and his brother Bob were reputed rumrunners during the 1920's. They were the earliest owners of the Old Mill when it became a tavern. (Captain Naugles also flew a plane which was used to spot Federal Agents.) By about 1930, Stanley left Bob at the Old Mill and moved next door to open the Anchor Inn. The Anchor Inn went on to become a very popular restaurant along with the Old Mill. The Anchor burned down in 1977 and was never rebuilt. James Boscola took over the Old Mill from the Naugles family, but Richard Holmes and his wife operated it from 1958 to 1975. For the past eleven years, Judy and Jerry Daly have continued the tradition of the Old Mill Inn.

The Old Mill, 1911
Mattituck Inlet

The Anchor Inn, 1939
Mattituck Inlet

Prohibition and the North Fork Restaurants

After World War I, the powerful Women's Christian Temperance Association seemed to have won the age-old battle against alcohol. Prohibition, or more exactly, the Volstead Act, went into effect in January 1923. Robert Carse, author and sea captain from Shelter Island, wrote a book, *Rum Row*, in 1959. In it he describes the chaotic but economically thriving days of prohibition on the North Fork. I believe that these events influenced the taverns in our area, many of which evolved into full service restaurants. The following quotes are from *Rum Row*:

Greenport in the 1920's was a town of indiscriminate architecture where, upon two streets, the stores, a movie theater, a restaurant or so, a few garages, a pair of bowling alleys, a sailmaker and a chandlery served the residents and the neighboring fishermen, farmers, and summer folk. The bootleggers, in collusion with the rum-runners, took it over after dark ...

Most of the town's population of less then ten thousand derived some form of profit from their disregard of the Prohibition law. Unemployment was practically non-existent. Men strong enough to carry a case of liquor were hired and paid an average of twenty dollars a night to transfer the loads from the contact boats to the waiting trucks. The boatyards were busy at work on craft for which no contracts had been drawn but none were needed: everything the rum-runners ordered done was on a cash-in-advance basis ...

The trucks came in from New York with the approach of darkness. They were accompanied by the cars that would form the escort on the return, usually gray Buick touring cars ... The trucks formed in carefully aligned columns as soon as they were loaded for the more than one-hundred mile run to New York. The scout cars moved ahead with a bevy of hoodlums in each, Thompson guns across the knees ...

Taverns flourished on the North Fork during Prohibition. Food was gradually added and perhaps some entertainment on Saturday night. Picturesque, out of the way locations such as the Old Mill in Mattituck became very popular. This popularity and business structure carried over into the post World War II era. The stories were told and retold over the years, and trap doors from bootlegging days were savored as proof of past events. The personality and color has survived to this day.

Four Doors Down
Half Shell West
The Apple Tree
Half Shell Republic
The Coach Stoppe
The Coach House
The Apple Tree

Main Road
Mattituck

The Apple Tree was probably the best known youth hang-out east of Smithtown during the 1950's and 60's. It has evolved with the times from a take-out food stand/bar of the 1930's to a high energy night club. During the summers of 1963 and 1964, the Kingsmen performed here before their hit "Louie Louie" took them to national fame. More recently, it has been a popular family dining spot and sports bar. Skip's Deli (added on to the Apple Tree in 1971) was probably the first deli on the North Fork. Since 1971 this building has been the center of operations for one of the area's most successful restaurateurs, Skip Schoenhaur. With the help of his wife Phyllis and partners Bob Schoenhaur and Carroll Harvey, Skip has owned and operated the Dry Dock and Doc's Tavern in Riverhead; Little Joe's in Aquebogue; The Galley Ho in New Suffolk; The Coach Stoppe in Mattituck; Skip's Deli; and the Mill Creek Inn in Southold. He also operated the Noyack Country Club.

For Skip, it began with a bartending job at the General Wayne after college. He would close up at night all alone and walk in the pitch dark between the evergreens through the backyard with the cash box, saying out loud "I'll throw the money on the ground and keep walking." This is how he learned about cash control.

By listening to the right people, by keeping close watch on payroll and product costs, and by keeping his ego in check, Skip has mastered the often elusive goal of running a profitable restaurant on the North Fork. Successfully operating multiple restaurants in our area is very rare.

Whether it was bringing entertainment such as Jimmy Digons or Stonehill to the Coach Stoppe, keeping the rustic look of the Galley Ho, or serving hugely popular breakfasts at Skip's Deli, his style of maintaining local color and ambiance has contributed to the character of the North Fork.

1936

THE APPLE TREE
Jericho Turnpike
MATTITUCK, L. I., N. Y.
(90 Miles from New York City)

DINNERS SERVED

Toasted Sandwiches

Hot Roast Beef	.35
Hot Pastrami on Rye	.20
Frankfurter and Sauerkraut	.10
Hamburger, Spanish Onion	.10
Hamburger, Butter-fried Onions	.15
Hamburger DeLuxe	.20
Ham	.15
Egg	.10
Peanut Butter and Bacon	.20
Ham and Peanut Butter	.20
Lettuce and Tomato	.15
Ham, Lettuce and Tomato	.20
Bacon, Lettuce and Tomato	.30
Western	.20
Grilled Bacon	.15
American or Swiss Cheese	.15
Cream Cheese and Jelly	.20
Grilled Olde English Cheese	.20
Olde English Cheese and Ham	.25
Olde English Cheese and Tomato	
Olde English Cheese and Bacon	

PIE FROM OUR OWN OVENS

Reid's Ice Cream

Coffee (pure cream) .05   Tea .10   Milk .10

Coffee Served in Cars .10

SCHLITZ ON DRAUGHT

The Red Door
The Heritage Inn
The Western Sunset
The Main Road Tavern
The Lobster Pot
Villa D'oro
Sundown

Main Road
Mattituck

This former private home was turned into a high energy bar in the mid-'70s called Sundown. After a few years it was purchased by the Catugno family and transformed into an elegant Northern Italian restaurant called Villa D'oro. It featured a marble bar, a vintage Cadillac limousine and valet parking. Perhaps a little too upscale for the North Fork then, it was turned into a more local concept called The Lobster Pot. After brief runs as a tavern and a steakhouse it became The Heritage Inn, featuring local ingredients and international recipes.

It is now The Red Door. Chef owner Stephan Mazella came from Manhattan in 2001 with a rich professional background. He cooked for La Cote Basque, L'Espinasse, and The Four Seasons Hotel. He represents a new generation of chefs who are talented, skilled, and college educated. Stephan watches the stock market as closely as he watches the stock pot.

His menu is a good example of how the North Fork restaurant has evolved over the years. Each dish is a self-contained work of art, mixing colors, textures, flavors, and aromas as if from an artist's palette. Pan seared sea scallops with jade pesto, spaghetti squash, toasted pine nuts ... the elements are simple and fresh, incorporating local ingredients in season. A typical menu of the late '60s had 28 entrees, 22 appetizers and soups, 19 sandwiches, 7 salads and 11 desserts. Instead of an orchestrated plate, your entree came with a foil-wrapped baked potato or French fries and a monkey dish of steam table vegetables. Contemporary menus run the risk of becoming too eclectic — many foods are best when handled the least — but they give a chef the opportunity to create a sensual experience that goes beyond ordinary food.

Portobello Ristorante
The Wine Garden
The Hut

Route 48
Mattituck

In 1989 James Duffy bought this property, which had once been a hot dog stand called The Hut. Jim was a graduate of the New York Restaurant School and had worked at Sam's Restaurant in Rockville Centre. He renovated the building into a beautiful fine dining restaurant surrounded by trees and grape vines. It was called the Wine Garden. Jim Duffy operated it until 1997 when he decided to pursue a career in financial management. In 2002, veteran restauranteur Diane Walters moved the Portobello Ristorante from Greenport to this property in Mattituck.

A Touch of Venice
Matt-A-Mar Snack Bar

Matt-A-Mar Marina
Mattituck

Ettore Pennacchia, his wife Barbara and son Brian opened their restaurant on Mattituck Inlet in 1988. An Italian American who loves to cook, he began with Ettore's Italian cuisine in Selden and moved to the North Fork, establishing his signature use of local ingredients with an Italian/Mediterranean style.

Years ago, a few Italian restaurants enjoyed a local following of regulars who enjoyed clams oreganata, pasta with marinara sauce, and lasagna. Thirty years later, Ettore offers eggplant sorrentino, fried calamari insalata, risotto con granchio, and rosemary roasted duck with butternut squash gnocchi. These dishes are accompanied by some of the North Fork's best wines. His customers are a new generation with sophisticated taste and a love of the North Fork.

209

Do Little's
Café Mediterranean

Main Road
Mattituck

T he North Fork is known more for its historic buildings and endless miles of waterfront than for its shopping centers. Usually the only restaurants in these locations are pizza and Chinese take-out.

Chef/owner Frank Purita and his Italian born wife, Chef Claudia Fruci, went against the grain when they opened the very upscale Café Mediterranean in 1994. The entry and store front were small, located next door to the supermarket. But the restaurant opened up in the back with a large, beautifully decorated dining room. The food was excellent, with homemade pastries and Mediterranean cuisine that many North Fork people weren't familiar with. They also had an ambitious wine list. Perhaps the restaurant was a little too ambitious for the location — it closed within two years.

Do Little's and Victorian Catering have survived the test of time as a casual restaurant/sports bar and a successful catering business.

Old Bohemian Café
Savan's
Wishbone Inn
Jim's Diner

Main Road
Mattituck

Storied Past
This building, located on Main Road in Mattituck, has undergone many reincarnations since it looked this way in the early 1970s. Its next stint may come as a café specializing in German cuisine.

Many small restaurants on the North Fork began as snack bars, luncheonettes, or diners. Over the years they would acquire new owners who made renovations and the building would evolve into something more complex.

This building was very popular as Jim's Diner in the 1970's but has spent most of the time since then boarded up. In 1977, Mary Lozinski sold it to James Naza. In the early 1980's a bar was added in the rear and the name changed to the Wishbone Inn. It then began a brief tenure as the upscale Savan's featuring continental cuisine. After being closed for a long period, Rudy Fadeley bought it and hoped to open the Old Bohemian Café. Rudy originally came from the Czech Republic and planned to serve lots of goulash, bratwurst and beer. The restaurant never opened.

In the old days, opening a restaurant was uncomplicated and pretty inexpensive. But as time moves on the rules become more complex and the expenses much greater. The saga of the Old Bohemian Café emphasizes what a restauranteur must overcome to pursue the dream. First the basics: Adequate cesspools that meet health department standards; fire safety and handicap access; adequate parking and current legal zoning. Next the financing (the purchase price is only the beginning): Renovations, new equipment; unexpected expenses; costly delays. And finally the marketing: In a very competitive seasonal environment, why are customers going to be attracted to your place? And if they are, what will keep them coming back for more? The overused cliché — "It's a tough business" — has never been more true. But you have to admire the men and women who overcome the obstacles and pursue their dreams, making our neighborhood an exciting place to live.

Mattituck Buildings
That Were Once Restaurants

Chez Nous
The Candle Light Inn

Main Road

Razmataz
The Captains Quarters

Main Road

North Fork Grill
Bella Notte
Ding How
Mattituck Diner

Main Road

The Tolendal Inn

Main Road

Blue Water Seafood

Main Road

Jamesport and Aquebogue

Colby's
The Elbow Room

Route 25
Jamesport

As the name implies, the Elbow Room is a small restaurant. It started small in 1958 and it remains so today. It is also one of the most successful North Fork restaurants of the last 40 years.

It all began when Cliff Saunders Sr. opened the Laurel Inn (now the Elbow Too) in 1946. His son, Cliff Jr., was not in the tavern business at first, but after a number of other jobs he and his wife Joan bought a tavern on the Main Road in Jamesport and called it the Elbow Room. It was 1958. The building consisted of a bar and, in the present dining room, a pool table, dart board, and a shuffleboard court. At first only sandwiches were served.

By 1965 Cliff Jr. was buying steaks from the old A&P Supermarket in Mattituck, cooking chowder and making stuffed clams. He also developed a secret marinade for his steaks. His steak business grew rapidly. He was now buying short loins of beef from Jules Wicksman and he hired Gene Hiffliker as his butcher. He would cut porterhouse steaks and use all the trim for fresh hamburger. It became very difficult to get a table at the Elbow Room. The marinated steaks became famous (and much copied); the simple menu with modest prices and friendly service made Cliff's Restaurant a landmark institution on the North Fork.

215

In 1971, Cliff bought the Laurel Inn from his father and re-named it Elbow Too. Cliff's younger brother Frank was the bar-tender there for 40 years before he passed away in 2003. Cliff bought The Rendezvous in Riverhead in 1976. He also bought the old Seafarer in Southold in 1988 and eventually renamed it Cliff's Elbow East. Instead of expanding his original restaurant, Cliff chose to develop a mini-chain of small restaurants based on the same theme. His formula of simplicity and tight family man-agement worked. Cliff Saunders Jr. died in 2002. Management has passed to his son Cliff Saunders III and his wife Christina. Cliff's sister, Jean, is the manager of the Rendezvous and Cliff's mother Joan still makes chowder at the Elbow Room. They sold the Elbow East property to longtime employee Bill Berliner and his sister Katherine.

The Elbow Room captures the unique character of the North Fork. Its quaint style and long-time local following of farmers, fisherman and townspeople contributes much to our rural atmo-sphere. After 47 years, it is still going strong.

The Elbow Room, and Cliff
Saunders, Jr., 1958

The Bayview Inn

South Jamesport Ave.
Jamesport

According to Bob Patchell, in 1903 South Jamesport was another Atlantic City. There were two 100-room hotels, The Miamogue and The Great Peconic House, surrounded by boarding houses and small inns. One of these inns was The Bayview, completely renovated and re-opened by the Patchell family in 2002. When you visit a restored property like this on the North Fork, history comes alive. You picture families riding in horsedrawn carriages from the railway station a half mile away, settling into the hotel and relaxing on the veranda with a drink.

Speaking of drinks, it becomes very clear that bootlegging was a major industry on the North Fork during prohibition. The endless miles of difficult to navigate waterways combined with inns, hotels, and taverns that were off the beaten track made for a perfect setting. Then, as now, we were that hidden little gem not too far from New York City.

Bob and Pat Patchell have operated the Motel on the Bay for over 20 years. Now, with the help of their sons Scott and Gregory they are operating the Bayview Inn. It has seven rooms and two suites, a bar, and two dining rooms. The fine dining menu includes tuna tartare, clams fra diavolo, braised rabbit, crescent duck, and lobster stew.

The Bayview Inn

The Great
Peconic House

The Miamogue

Captain Dimon House
Twin Oaks
Jamesport Manor Inn

Manor Lane
Jamesport

This nostalgic old piece of North Fork history was originally built as the home of Captain James Dimon in the 1850's. He was a whaling captain and reputed to be the founder of Jamesport hamlet. Not too surprisingly, the house was believed to be haunt-
ed. It began its history as a commercial establishment as Twin Oaks. At one time there were cabins in the back which were rented to tourists. Like other old North Fork

establishments, its history around Prohibition is a little shadowy.

In more recent times, a former Grumman engineer, Neal Kopp, ran the restaurant as the Jamesport Manor Inn for 20 years. It was known for its Long Island duck, its sauerbraten and its country inn atmosphere.

**Jamesport Country
Kitchen
Village Coffee Pot**

**Route 25
Jamesport**

The Jamesport Country Kitchen has never been a high profile trendy restaurant, nor has its owner, Matt Kar, ever been a "celebrity" chef. But Matt has balanced the artistic and financial demands of the North Fork like a master. From the time he bought it in 1987, he has built its reputation as a quality North Fork restaurant with a casual ambiance and moderate prices. He embraced Long Island wines early, used fresh local ingredients and captured the unique personality of our area.

In 1994 Matt Kar was the first local restaurateur to identify the market for weddings and other events at the wineries. People wanted to get married in a vineyard and Matt responded by developing Christopher Michael Catering. He added refrigerated trucks and a catering kitchen behind his restaurant and watched the business grow every year until its sales equalled those of his restaurant.

Matt is now restoring the old Jamesport Manor Inn to its former glory and will be opening it as a restaurant soon.

The Modern Snack Bar

Route 25
Aquebogue

The historic North Fork is the last rural outpost on Long Island, a little old-fashioned but less pretentious than the Hamptons, and inhabited by friendly honest people. When you pass the Modern Snack Bar in Aquebogue, with its 1950's neon sign and unassuming building, you know you've entered the North Fork.

The Modern Snack Bar opened as Al McGee's Snack Bar in 1949 with a counter and a few stools. Wanda Wittmeier's sister Lilian worked for Al McGee and took over in 1950. Wanda joined her in 1952 and, with her husband John, bought the business in 1956. The family has operated it ever since, with brothers Otto and John now in charge. The "Snack Bar" has evolved into a full service restaurant.

The old sign reminds you that it has a long history, that change doesn't take place quickly, and that the prices are modest. The menu reflects both the foods of the North Fork and its personality: lobster salad plate; roast Long Island duck; slow cooked pork loin; sauerbraten with red cabbage; and stuffed flounder. In a stroke of marketing genius, the Modern Snack Bar has turned the lowly turnip into a signature attraction along with old fashioned baked pies.

In an era of restaurant chains, convenience stores, and very high end fine dining restaurants, Otto and John Wittmeier have faced the challenges of running a successful business without losing the simple quality of the past. A family operated restaurant over fifty years old is a remarkable achievement.

Vineyard Caterers
Brasby's
Knob Hill

Route 25
Aquebogue

Advertisement,
1972

Bill Brasby dominated the on-premise catering business on the west end of the North Fork during the 1970's and 1980's. He had seating for at least 300, a large kitchen, and plenty of parking. The buffet was the most popular style of service and his food specialty was steamboat roast beef. This consisted of an entire leg, or round of beef, including the shank. It would be slow roasted for about 12 hours and placed upright under a heat lamp for carving. The rest of the buffet consisted of a salad bar and chafing dishes containing sausage and peppers, baked ziti, and stuffed flounder. Prices were low and the portions very large.

Brasby's was sold and completely renovated into a catering facility specializing in weddings. It is now called Vineyard Caterers.

Fauna
Hans Gasthaus
Little Joe's

Route 25
Aquebogue

During the 1970's and 1980's, Little Joe's was the most popular Italian Restaurant on the North Fork. Before the revolution in regional Italian cuisine began, Joe and his wife Kay served a simple menu of spaghetti with marinara sauce, baked lasagne and ziti, clams oreganata and Italian style cheesecake. No pizza. Joe worked behind the small bar and Kay was the hostess. They lived behind the restaurant and were open for dinner only. Their formula for a successful business was simplicity. A simple menu with consistent quality and very moderate prices; a small staff and reasonable hours of operation. They would close for a month in the winter for vacation.

After Joe retired, the restaurant became Hans Gasthaus, featuring knockwurst, bratwurst, sauerkraut and Austrian specialties, and a bar with many European beers.

In about 2000 the restaurant was expanded and renamed Fauna. A catering facility replaced the living quarters in back and the menu went upscale with the "New American Cuisine."

The Meeting House Creek Inn
The Poop Deck

Meeting House Creek Road
Aquebogue

Beginning as a tackle/bait shop attached to a marine supply store, this building became a bar serving light food in 1967. It was called the Poop Deck. Larry and Arline Galasso bought the marina in 1970 and have leased out the restaurant ever since.

Tom Drake became the tenant in 1989, changing the name to the Meeting House Creek Inn. His wife Leslie is his pastry chef and Phil Giacalone, a graduate of Johnson and Wales Culinary School, his long time chef. Tom worked for years at the Pine Grove Inn in Patchogue before managing Baron's III in Bohemia and owning the Senix Creek Inn in Center Moriches.

The Meeting House Creek Inn is a marina restaurant that is open year round and has a good following of local residents. The menu is fairly extensive, with many North Fork favorites. Sauerbraten and grilled bratwurst reflect Tom's experience at the Pine Grove Inn. Duck from Crescent across the street, local seafood, and marinated steaks let you know you're on the North Fork.

Recipe Index

Restaurant Index by Town
Most Recent Names Only